DuJuan S Boyd

MARRIAGE
of Pearls
God's Design
for a Healthy Marriage

Marriage of Pearls

God's Design for a Healthy Marriage

DuJuan Boyd

Pure Thoughts Publishing, LLC

Marriage of Pearls

All Scripture quotation, unless otherwise indicated, are taken from the Holy Bible, New International Version®. NIV®. Copyright © 1973, 1978, 1984 by International Bible Society. Used by permission of Zondervan Publishing House. All rights reserved.

ISBN: 978-1-943409-12-9

Table of Contents

Dedication

This book is very special to me as I found my first love in high-school. We were in-between periods at school and during those days we would have dance offs and as I was dancing and rocking to the beat and during a double spin, a spin that would change my life forever a spin that instantly, I felt my heart was connecting to the beat of this beautiful young lady that sat on the floor of the hall watching me dance. I was drawn to her like a magnet to metal, like a string to a guitar, like the keys to a keyboard. I pulled her from the floor in the heat of it all, our hearts were racing, we were breathing a mile a minute, as our breaths began to make their own rhythm, I could feel our bodies getting closer and closer and our souls instantly became one at that very moment we were soul-mates and didn't even know it…   We became the only ones in the hallway yet there were at least 45 people around watching us connect in love/unity that is very rare these days. This woman has been my rock, my love, my support, together we have battled the world and overcame everything that has come our way, even during the time we had no place to live, but we had 2 children to take care, no jobs, and no transportation, we began to get closer spiritually, making us even stronger through God and without this woman, my life wouldn't be in the place it is in today, I wouldn't have the drive I have, I wouldn't be married, I surely wouldn't be witting this book on marriage…

Through the years, we've faced many test, many trials, we've had ups and downs, good times and bad times but through it all we've come out with more substance than when we first went into the test and trials and we overcome those storms with God first, understanding each other, talking and not yelling, giving each other space when needed, finding time to pray together, worshipping together and making time to have date nights. Regardless of your schedule you have to make time for each other in every way possible…

I dedicate this book to my beautiful wife as she sits in her chair relaxing, looking great as ever and her name is Jackie K Boyd, she is my rib, my soul-mate, my everything in this world and to have a love like this is to have heaven everyday…

DuJuan S Boyd

Introduction

Statistically most of you reading this book will be married in a relatively short time. Now for some, they're reading this saying "I'm scared!!!   Am I ready? Is this really the one for me, what if this doesn't work out?"

Then there are others who will read this smiling not thinking or worrying about any of those other things above, because they just want to be married at any/all cost and in most cases we will get married with no counseling or even run to the court house to be wed, just to say we did it...

Sad truth is that we also see in our culture today that unless you do something different than what everyone else is doing right now, no more than half of the people reading this book will stay married longer than 2 years... That is why God gave me this book written by the Holy Spirit, because he wants/needs healthy marriages, spirit lead marriages, and happy marriages. God needs a marriage where he is the head of the marriage, not the tail and a marriage without God is a marriage on the road to destruction!!!

You must have a standard in what you want/need your marriage to be and not accept anything less walking into the marriage, make it known upfront the way the marriage should be and that you will not be the spare tire waiting in the trunk when the girlfriend/boyfriend is blown out... Let it be known upfront that you won't be the gasoline can waiting in the garage alone in a corner collecting dust, forgotten about only used when your spouse has ran out of gas, stranded on the side of the road and needs a fill up…

I challenge you as you read this book, that you take your thoughts and make them God's thoughts, based on the scriptures in this book and I promise you it will completely transform how we think about/look at marriage, it will transform the way you interact and see the married people around you in your life, It will transform your thoughts on what it is you think you are looking for in a marriage and a spouse.
It is great to have everything in your fairytale wedding you like, but it is even greater to have everything you need for your marriage to survive...

Chapter 1

"Women, Protect your pearls against the Swine"

Matthew 7:6-"Do not give dogs what is sacred; do not throw your pearls to pigs. If you do, they may trample them under their feet, and turn and tear you to pieces.

We see here in this text God gives instructions on protecting your pearls and keeping them Holy. The first instruction is:

1.) "Don't give dogs what is sacred" My question to you all reading this book. "What is Sacred to you? What dogs have you let in your yard? What in your life have you let dogs destroy? Do you have a dog that respects you? Does the dog love you? Why Is God using dog as a metaphor? When dogs are man's best friend.

Let us first understand that dogs were apart of society, but were half wild and roamed the region in packs that were sometimes dangerous to humans. The word dogs used here refers specifically to dogs without a master, no home training, just downright nasty and un-controllable.

You can't marry someone who wants still roam the streets and hang out in clubs as if they want to still be single in life, they must first see their issues and problems and begin to work towards correcting the issues, problems and start to put away their old ways, become more mature and none of this is possible if they are not renewed in Christ and serve him as Lord and Savior in their life.

The dogs were known for being unclean and would eat whatever scraps and carrion they came across.

Stop trying to be with someone that you know is unclean and you know is sleeping around with every other person in the city and wants to come home and lay with you after rolling around in dirt, eating trash that possibly has maggots in it and they end up bringing home the flees and whatever dirty virus they've picked up in the streets of lust and suddenly you find yourself in tears crying to God with aloud voice for help while trying to figure out why you're in the hospital sick, vomiting, feverish, sweating and on life support.

Leave those dogs alone because they will only rip your heart out your chest and most dogs think they are the master of you and will try to control you at all cost even if that means barking scriptures at you to get you to submit, biting you with words of hatred to break you down to lower your self-esteem in life or even scratching/hitting you with their paws of anger and with each blow you become weaker, with each blow you become helpless, with each blow you fall into depression, with each blow your knees get weaker and before you know it you have bowed your whole life to a person that cares nothing about you and only wants to control you to benefit their not wanting to be alone and subdue and hide their issues they had as a child.

2.) "Don't throw your pearls to pigs." Pigs are the quintessential unclean and when Jesus cast the legion of demons out of the man in Mark 5:1-13 we see that Jesus cast the demons into the pigs and the pigs In Verse 13 ran into the lake by the thousands and drowned.

Pigs are a class of humans that can't appreciate religion, life, love, family or marriage, let alone appreciate you and the love you have to offer them. Pigs are set apart from other animals because they are so unclean and they roll around in slop, dirt, mud all day long and they are not comfortable or happy unless they are in that environment of nastiness.

Which further means you can't marry a person who has the thought life and physical life of a pig because they are unclean with all kinds of bad spirits on them. One day they are happy and the next day they are at your throat because you're not dirty enough for them and you're not good enough for them, nothing you do is good enough, food is nasty, sex is bad, juice is sour, the sugar is not sweet, your meat has no flavor to them, your lips are not worthy to touch theirs, the house isn't clean enough, you're not trusted, certain parts of your body are not worthy to even be eaten by the mater so parts of you are thrown aside to the less fortunate in life and you become devoured, closed in, trapped, unhappy, unwanted, unloved and in your own house you feel like a slave In a mud box of slop and everywhere you turn you're falling in mud amongst the pigs that are trashing your home and marriage.

If you're not careful the spirits that are upon the spouse "Pig" you've married/thinking of marrying they will run your life completely in the lake and destroy you by drowning you with their filthiness and demonic spirits that have come only to destroy/hinder your life.

The common denominator of the Dogs and Pigs is destruction of your life and marriage...

Or you'll be living in a marriage of Swine Flu just waiting and watching the clock for the day of destruction because without God there is no cure for your pearls that have been tainted by the swine you've chosen to keep in your life.

<u>"Please know that your pearls are a luxury and are of extreme value that money can never buy"</u>.

If Jesus tells us that it is unhealthy to eat of the swine, why then do you think/want/need to marry the swine??? Do you love and enjoy slop that much???

These animals will even come into your life portraying to know and love Jesus and will say anything to get you to lay out your pearls before them. They will tell you that they love you, they will tell you that you are the greatest thing that has ever happened to them, they will play the role buying you nice things, rings, clothes, shoes and even take you to the best restaurants in the world "under their budget" trying to get into the bank after hours and if the pearls are still not unlocked from the safe deposit box, they will even ask you to marry them with the only intention of destroying your royal pearls.

Once you've said yes to the proposal, the pressure is on then to give up the pearls and most will even use scriptures to say that it is ok to open the box of pearls just so they can see what the pearls look like. To see if they are rare, if they are shinning, if they are worth buying and most only care about the shape and not what's truly inside this rare pearl...

They will even become power struck; it is either their way or no way at all. The true pig begins to come out once you've said yes to the pig and while you are all in your emotions you don't see the pig/dog standing before you, all you see is the ultimate life, dream of happiness and love.

As the days go by you start to see the change in the pig, the smell of the pig, the nastiness of the pig and there Is no more dinner dates, no rings, no clothes you can't even spend your own money in the way or form that you desire which makes you a slave to their will and in your own home.

Marriage of Pearls

So, now you are thinking if you should follow through with the wedding or not but in most cases by this point you are in too deep!!!

"So you think"

You've given up your pearls!!! You have a baby with the swine!!! We all know that no pig takes care of their children!!! So you are stuck handling the load alone... You can't even figure out how to get the swine out of your house!!! You start to feel closed in!!! Nowhere to turn, no one to call on because you don't want to be judged of saying yes and months later saying no... All you do now is beat yourself up because the last thing you wanted to do is fail at anything your parents failed at and that pressure of not wanting to marry to divorce is building up your blood pressure and now your veins are pumping rapidly with each day and at any given moment you will be boiling over in anger, frustration and envy not understanding that there is a propensity to allow these spirits to rest inside of you. You are at the point of a nervous breakdown, you're losing your hair and you can't sleep at night, you toss and you turn, you wake up soak and wet from sweating and you are feeling tired because you've been fighting this marriage/relationship all in your sleep about this pig trying to destroy your pearls.

You begin to want out of the slop box of mud and everything that the pig does irritates you and you will start the smallest arguments just to leave the house to feel free again from the curse this demon has brought in your home and in most cases you don't even want to go home or you will sit in the drive way in your car praying and crying because there is a dormant spirit of depression that lives there and there is no peace in your own home because where ever the pig goes their friends go as well.

So, now you have a house full of demon filled pigs and they're trashing up your home, your life, eating all your food and when they leave, they leave the house trashed, nasty, the odor of your home makes you sick to your stomach and you start to now feel empty inside because you can't even get restoration in your own home and all your belongings have been tainted by the swine you let in your home.

To protect your pearls you must know what they are and what they are worth…

➢ The worldly pearl is tiny sandstone that finds its way under an oyster shell, and it starts irritating the oyster and the oyster begins to work on the stone, and soon one day this sandstone becomes this beautiful, smooth, shiny pearl. These pearls in the world can cost humans thousands to millions of dollars because it takes a lot of small pearls to make up one necklace or bracelet. They are so hard to get/find that they become priceless to those who owns or finds one.

➢ The spiritual pearl- Jesus is telling us in a parable in the book of Matthew, of a merchant looking for fine pearls and referred this to finding the kingdom of heaven and that when you find the kingdom of heaven, your salvation is like a precious pearl!!!

Matthew 13:45-46 says,

"Again the kingdom of heaven is like a man who is a dealer in search of fine and precious pearls, who, on finding a single pearl of great price, went and sold all he had and bought it."

Marriage of Pearls

That tells us that your pearls are as precious as the kingdom of heaven and you shouldn't just toss your soul around to evil people/spirits and you will know the right spouse to give your pearls to because that person will give up everything for you...

They will give up their past hurt, love, pain, issues, addictions, streets, clubs, drinking; money, lust, flesh and they will not control you or manipulate your mind. They will give up everything they love to be with you and if that person is not willing to leave everything behind them to be with you, then you might want to reconsider the marriage/relationship you are in right now because it will only end in divorce for you and you will find yourself in the dating game all over again hoping to find life's promise of true love, broken, crying with tainted and stolen pearls you can never get back.

The real/true love of your life will hold your smooth pearls while you're in pain and never place pain upon you... They will make sure that you shine in every way and not throw dirt on you, you will have case of your own in their heart, soul and life and not in the oceans of a phonebook filled with leaches, sharks, snakes, alligators or stingrays looking to destroy you or your marriage.

No other jewel will matter because they will have given up everything to be with you and they'll hold you so close that there is no room for another jewel to come in-between you two because your pearls will be as precious to him as a soul is to God!!!

"Protect your pearls from the start!!!"

Chapter 2

"The Charge to the Husbands"

Ephesians 5:25-"Husbands, love your wives, just as Christ also loved the church and gave Himself up for her,"

Let's look at the first part… "Husbands, Love your wives" This a direct instruction from God for men to love their wives, not only saying it but love here is an action word and should be shown to your wives that you love them…
How do you know if you love your wife the way God has ordered you to???

(1) Are you kind to her even when it hurts? This means putting your own feelings to the side in an argument and placing her feelings first… You should be the person to fix the issue rather than add fuel to the issue because the more gas added to the fire; it will only cause the fire to spread and the bigger the fire the greater the damage…

(2) Are you envious of her talent or gifts, or her intelligence? Men tend to get bitter and angry because the woman has more talents and gifts than he does and maybe smarter and hold more college degrees than he does, but in no way should the man hold her achievements in life against her because she decided to better herself and you decided to stay the same in the same place in life and you are ok with working your 9 to 5 making minimum wage at the warehouse and you depend on her to pay all the bills while you keep your money in your pockets…

Instead, never get comfortable where you are in life!!! "Living to just get by should never be an option in life!" Always strive to do better in life!!! Push yourself to run your own business!!! Become the bread winner in the household!!! Put your gifts and talents together to make things better in the household!!! Who cares who makes more!!! You are one and the money comes together to make an increase in the home!!!

(3) **Do you consider yourself smarter or better than her in any way?**

(4) **Are you rude to her?**

(5) **Can she count on the fact that you will do without in order to put her first?**

(6) Does she have to walk on "eggshells" around you or is she comfortable being herself?

(7) **Does it make you happy when she fails or is embarrassed by something or someone?**

(8) **Are you patient with her?**

(9) **Do you make every effort for her succeed in every area of her life?**

(10) **Are you flirtatious with other women?**

(11) **Is she treated as your equal or as your child?**

The man is to be the woman's rock, her shield, her protector, the lover of all her desires, he is to meet every need of her life, support her dreams and guide her with love, shower her with gifts just because to make her smile, don't just offer flowers when you've done something wrong offer up a rose from your soul daily to stay connected her feelings…

So many men run from marriage because they are scared of the pain from the passion that marriage will bring because they don't want to be hurt, so they put themselves into a cave and hide themselves from the woman they love for fear of being hurt… Not understanding that it is the cave that they hide in that keeps them from being the man she needs them to be…

But, how can the man be the man of the marriage and do what the lord has asked him to do if most of the men in the world are being dominated by their wives with every step they take???

I am sure if there were signs in heaven on judgment day one would read, "All men that have been controlled/abused/dominated by your wives please stand here!" I am certain that that line would stretch as far as the heavens begins and ends because the roll of the man in most households have become powerless or even non-existent in the home…

We even hear men in the church standing before a large congregation on men's day and say things like, "I wear the pants in my household!" All the while the wife is seating there with a smug look on her face like yeah right!!! The reality of this is that who is the man of the house is no laughing matter and should never have to be expressed in public, it is something that you just walk in and be…

Most men fall into this category because they are confused and insecure and most men were never even taught how to express their love to the woman without finding fault or issues in the woman. They've never had the male leadership guidance in the home to provide them with a model of what a man should be and do… Thus leaving no mental picture of what it takes or how to even lead a family let alone be a great husband to his wife and in return leaves the woman feeling un-loved, insecure, unwanted, unhappy leading to her wanting to undo her vows to the man she fell in love with because the man is not leading the home effectively in the right direction and in most cases the man doesn't even try to lead the family…

With most of these men not knowing or having a relationship with their fathers and they also don't have a relationship with God the

Marriage of Pearls

father and Christ must be the head of every man and if he doesn't know God the father then that man can't even lead himself in the right direction, so if God is not head of the man's life then there is no way that this man can be the head of the woman's life and the woman will never let the man lead her or the family if she can't trust him to do lead effectively in the right direction…

(1 Corinthians 11:3). Wives, be subject to your own husbands, as to the Lord. The husband is the head of the wife/household, as Christ also is the head of the church, He Himself being the Savior of the body. But as the church is subject to Christ, so also the wives ought to be to their husbands in everything. Husbands, love your wives, just as Christ also loved the church and gave Himself up for her, so that He might sanctify her, having cleansed her by the washing of water with the word, that He might present to Himself the church in all her glory, having no spot or wrinkle or any such thing; but that she would be holy and blameless. So husbands ought also to love their own wives as their own bodies. He who loves his own wife loves himself; for no one ever hated his own flesh, but nourishes and cherishes it, just as Christ also does the church, because we are members of His body…

This text gives men direct orders from God to husbands to treat the wife with love as Christ loved the Church and gave his life for the church and likewise men are to give their all to their wives even if it means death to the husband…

Never cause her pain because to cause her pain Is to cause yourself pain, husband are never to inflict pain purposely just to make the woman feel the pain that they feel, instead husband are to shield the woman from the pain and absorb the pain she feels when possible… To hate your wife is to hate yourself, so you are to love your life with all love, respect, honor through sickness and health, richer or poorer until death do you part because to love her means you love yourself…

(Ephesians 5:22-30)

We see here that God placed the ultimate responsibility with respect to the household on the shoulders of the husband . . . The Lord has assigned the wife the duty of obeying her husband yet. . This obedience must be a voluntary submission on her part and not forced by the man for her to do so through scriptures and yelling to his wife to get her to submit and she is only to submit her own husband, not to every man." So, if you have not placed a ring on her finger, don't try to get her to submit because the bible is clear that she is to submit only to her husband and no other man in the world...

This scripture was never meant to for man to use it as a tool to lure it over a woman's head to get her to submit and dominate her to get to adhere to his every command and need... Women should never be treated as the butt of a marriage under the man or behind the man because the bible clears stats that we are equal and should be treated as equals...

The man should respect his wife, not degrade her with abusive words in an attempt to break her self-esteem or being insensitive to her needs, feelings and her hearts desires...

Men should do as Adam did with Eve and receive your wives as a gift with great value to God and to him... Which means you should never neglect your wives because when you do, you force the wife to go find significance outside the marriage, thus pushing her outside the will of God, not only do you hurt her, you her yourself and you are outside the will of God for your marriage.

Men you must be effective and great leaders in the home even when she is fighting, cussing and screaming at you… Should the woman do these things? Probably not but we as men must stay strong and press on without arguing and leave that situation to God, give her time to cool down, even if that means going to another room for a while and approach her calmly asking her if she is ready to talk… Never leave any issue un-talked about because that issue that is not addressed can be the issue/thing that destroys your marriage…

Paul says the same to everyone. God has placed the husband in the position of responsibility. It does not matter what kind of personality a man may have. Your wife may be resisting you, fighting you, and spurning your attempts to lead, but it makes no difference. I believe our wives want us and need us to lead. You are not demanding this position; on the contrary, God placed you there. You will not lead her perfectly, but you must care for your wife and family by serving them with perseverance.

There were 3 ways husbands are called to love and lead their wives in servant-leadership:

1. The husband is called to model and demonstrate sacrificial, Christ like love toward her, (Ephesians 5:25). He should not be passive, but should accept the responsibility that God has given him as the leader in his marriage. He should look to Jesus as the perfect example of a great husband. Jesus gave up everything for His bride, the church. Following this example, the husband should lay down not just his physical life (i.e. take a bullet for her), but lay down his needs and desires for HERS daily.

2. The husband is to lead her spiritually, courageously helping her grow in her love and knowledge of the gospel and God's word, (Ephesians 5:26-27). This does not mean he is her "head" as some abusive men will insist, or that a wife gets her personal, spiritual strength from her husband. She gets her strength from God. It is not putting the husband in the place of Christ as if the husband is some sort of absolute authority…therefore, it does not mean putting the will of the husband before the will of Christ. It DOES mean he should pray for her and with her, and spur her on to love Jesus more than she loves even her husband.

3. The husband must joyfully serve and care for his wife the way he cares for his own body, (Ephesians 5:28-30).

- **What do the actions of a man look like?**

1. Be trustworthy – do what you say you will, consistently. Be a man of your word.

2. Make her load lighter, not heavier – ask her how you can do this.

3. Listen to her.

4. Pray for her and with her and your children, that they would love Jesus more than anything.

5. Put her needs ahead of yours.

6. Be a one-woman man – keep your eyes on her only and stay away from pornography.

7. Help her develop and use the gifts and abilities God gave her.

8. Help her fulfill her hopes and dreams; encourage her to be the woman God created her to be

9. Show her and TELL her you love her. Be her BEST encourager.

10. Sacrifice

Three Basic Things for Men:

1. Repent for the ungodly way of treating your wife

2. Believe in Jesus, trust him, and ask for His help

3. Bleed (like Jesus did on the cross) and Lead your wife in servant-leadership

Never treat your wife with disrespect or behave selfishly or abuse her because this is not how God ordained a marriage to be or a woman to be treated and God is in true displeasure of the men treating the women in this manner and woman if God is not pleased with the way you are being treated, how can you then be pleased with the way your husband has been treating you???

Stop taking the abuse that the man is giving you, telling you that it is God's plan for the marriage and your life when God has already spelled out in the bible the plans he has for your life and the marriage you have said I do to....

"Men be leaders and not dictators of your marriage"

Chapter 3

Proverbs 27:19

"Understanding a man's heart to understand a man's pain"

When the Bible speaks of the human heart it is speaking of the thinking of a man, a man's will, a man's emotions or feelings, a man's conscience, or any given combinations of these. However, the word may also have reference to the whole inner being of man combining all these elements into the one whole that makes up the man.

- Proverbs 27:19 As in water face reflects face, So the heart of man reflects man

As in water face reflects face: This shows us the issues that most relationships/marriages face in the very beginning as you have many women who want to change the man to shape and mold them into what they want/need the man to be… Making the man fit into some places the man was never ordained by God to fit. That is why we have so many men who are married and are un-happy, spending more time in their man cave than with their spouse. The man has no outlet to scream and even if he does scream, most women don't understand that the man's scream is so silent the woman will never hear it and in most cases that is because the woman is so caught up in her emotions and issues that she can't even see his pain, depression and stress that is upon her king… Instead of the man holding the spouse, there are times when the man wants/needs to be held. Where is his shoulder to cry on? Who will wipe his tears? Who can he tell that he has been molested as a child? Yes, there are more boys molested as children than there are girls.

No one ever knows because the boy is always told by his father to suck it up and be a man!!! You better not cry!!! So, as the girls are taught at a young age to be wives, cook, clean and most have the wedding already planned out by the age of 12 and are able to speak out to their mothers, the boy is taught to play with games and to never cry, suppress your feelings…

So, the man is never prepared for marriage and shown how to be a husband let alone a father because he never grew up around his father and his whole family has a long line of divorces and un-healthy marriages…

The only way he can be a successful husband is if he forgets all he was taught/seen, stop letting his family and in most cases his mother direct his life and consume him as if he is still a child with most mothers marrying the son and not even know it thus the reason the Bible says in Genesis 2:24 Therefore shall a man leave his father and his mother, and shall cleave unto his wife: and they shall be one flesh.

Marriage of Pearls

The word Cleave literally means to "leave and cleave" as "leave and be united" (NIV), "leave and be joined" This in its self can cause the trouble in the man's heart because we see here that he is made to choose between his parents and his wife and in most cases the father is nowhere around and it is no him choosing between the woman that gave him life and the woman that he is to become one flesh with for the rest of his life…

Mother's don't understand the pain they cause by not letting go of their sons, not letting go will cause all kinds of destruction in the marriage and in the family as a whole thus causing the man more pain in his heart seeing the destruction of his family on both sides…

Not fully leaving the parents to cleave to your wife will cause stress in the marriage and your wife will feel as if she is in competition with the mother and most women will not compete with any woman let alone your mother, so the man has to first truly commit to leave the parents and leaving the parents doesn't mean you can go see them or you have to ignore them, it simply means that you are honoring the word of God by becoming one with your wife and starting a family that Is to take higher priority over your parents and parents should honor the word of God in the same manor…

Likewise spouses have to learn to cleave to each other, if they don't the marriage will lack intimacy, unity and the will of God will not be in it and the end result will be destruction of the marriage…

The man here must first find out who he is by seeing his own face in the reflection of the water and not the face of someone that he desires not to be… The man must examine his own conscience, his heart, his soul, his mind, emotions and intentions in life… He must be able to see his own natural face in the glass that God has ordained just for him, the glass that God has created for him, the glass that God has given him to look in, the glass God has given him to drink from, the glass to discern the true character in himself to be the husband that God has ordained him to be and not the husband of his mother or the husband the wife wants to create him to be. He will never be the husband God has him to be if you keep placing the glass of your boyfriends in the past in his face wanting him to be the reflection of an old lover that you are still in love with. A man never wants to feel as if he is being measured up to other men especially a man that you are still in love with…

The man has to be lead by God and God alone so that he can ensure that he is leading his family in the right direction… As the bible says in Psalm 37:23 "The steps of a good man are ordered by the lord" this means that no one other than God can lead this man to his destiny no one can take through a short cut in life to get him where they want him to be because he needs the process to be a great husband as much as you need the promise that he will be a great husband for you, so if he is not allowed to go through that process that God has ordained for him, he will never find out who he is, he'll never learn to love himself, love God and the end result he will never be able to fully love you as his wife and you will be upset, angry and hurt because then you will think that he doesn't love you but how can he love you if he was never allowed to find himself, never allowed to love himself because he never found his self and by him not being allowed to find himself, he never found God and no man can love you without first loving God and worshipping God… Because he must love you as God so loved the church, which means sacrificing everything for you, even his life, but only the true love of God will allow him to do that for you…

Marriage of Pearls

Water in the scripture here serves as a mirror for the man looking into, reflecting the very essence of the man right down to the soul of that man and depending on what's in that man's heart at that time will determine what the water will reflect to the man... If it is evil spirits, he will evoke everyone that he comes into contact with and the same goes for him if it is a happy spirit that spirit will transfer to everyone he comes into contact with...

Now, if there are some issues in his past that are still causing him pain, that is what the water will reflect to him and all he will see is what happened to him in his past and he will run to his cave to be alone, hiding from the pain with feeling as if there Is no outlet for him to healed from this hurt he feels and the only outlet will be for him to play with his toys as he did as a kid.

Or will he see the pain that the world has placed on his shoulders, or the pain of not being able to be a man and provide for his family, or the pain of having a felony charge and not being able to get a job giving him thought s of going back to the street life to make money to feed his family??? We never stop to think why it is that Grandpa dies at least 10 years before Grandma is. This is in part of the fall of Adam in the garden through sin. The other added pressure is because the prophecy is in the male child... The Hebrew word Zeerah and all this affects a man's heart and mind...

The enemy is after the man because he knows to destroy the man is to destroy all mankind... So, men are constantly being hunted in this world, rather it be because of the color of their skin, the way they talk, dress or the most important the devil seeks to destroy him because he knows and sees the greatness in the man...

That's why when Jesus was born Joseph had to take him down into Egypt and hide him for 2 years because the enemy had a contract out to kill men, there was a decree to destroy every male child under 2 years old, he "Pharaoh" killed them young so there was chance for them to become kings... Men are on the hit list of the enemy!!!
Why are the men on the hit-list you say? Great question!!!!

They are on there because, in Genesis God told the devil---"I will put enmity (hatred, opposition) between thee and the woman, and between thy seed and her seed; it (the woman's seed) shall bruise thy head, and thou shalt bruise his heel" (Gen. 3:15).

This verse tells us that there will be ENMITY between the woman's seed (EVE) and the seed of the devil that deceived her... The word Enmity here literally means a blood feud, a constant never ending battle between the blood lines and the seed that the devil will try and destroy. He will stop at nothing to destroy the seed and that of the male bloodline...

God here promised that the serpent would fall to the seed of the woman, with that seed being Jesus Christ who then passed it on to all mankind to do greater works than he did. So, if you know that the woman can give birth to something that is going to destroy you, what then do you do as the devil? You seek to destroy every male child that is born and in this time frame between 2005-2016 we are losing our young teens to killings and no one understands why, it is because the evil spirits have over taken their minds, through entertainment, sex and clothing and the devil is destroying them, not one by one but, in large numbers daily...

The seed of the devil would be his spiritual descendants seeing that we fight not against flesh and blood but spiritual wickedness in high places... There are times in marriages or relationships where the man seems to feel, talk and look different and in most cases that is when he is overcome by so much that the spirits start to take over his mind and the more you ask him what's wrong the more he suppresses the issues deeper into his soul. He is only doing this to protect you as the man because he knows the struggle or spiritual hurt it can place on you by telling you everything he has going on in his head...

Proverbs 4:23

23 Keep thy heart with all diligence; for out of it are the issues of life.

Marriage of Pearls

Now to look into a man's heart... Am I talking about the actual heart that pumps blood and keeps you alive? Just as God isn't in this scripture, neither am I. I am talking about their psyche, their soul and their immaterial being. In most proverbs in the bible the heart is spoken of in the same manner.

It is the place of our character. What we think, feel, lust, passions, anger, envy, struggle, love, hate, rebel, deceive, become bitter, sad and In most cases depressed or stressed to the point of wanting to die...

The heart is not just the emotions of man; it is the whole inner soul, integrity and character of the man/woman... This is why we end up in bad relationships/marriages with men/women because we look at the man/woman on the outside, what they have, how they look, what they buy you, instead of looking at the whole heart of the man/woman which again is the whole inner being of a person...

"What is the heart of the man/woman you are marrying?"

Like women, men guard their hearts as well... "For out of it spring the issues of life."

Whatever is deep down inside a person is who they really are and if these things are not addressed up front during marriage counseling then the marriage will fail before it even starts and some men have so much hurt and pain built up inside of them from their childhood that they forget it is even there and will see no wrong in anything they do but, will always produce evil thoughts, lustful thoughts, angry words towards you, become murderers, adulteries, and these emotions and action can only rise from an evil heart that was once pure.

Matthew (5:8) says: "Only the pure in heart will see God" so, only the man that is pure in heart will see you for whom you are and love you as God loved the church...

The apostle Paul writes: Romans 8:6- [6] For to be carnally minded is death; but to be spiritually minded is life and peace.

The hearts of some men are so destroyed that they walk and talk carnally and think carnally and get married with a carnal mind causing death to the marriage before it even beings because they never dealt with that spirit, issues and pain from their past because no one has shown them how or even told them that it's there. Let's look at some things that can spring from a man's heart from the issues of life:

1.) **Not feeling/being adequate enough to take care of his family.** Let's face it, the roles have changed over the years and the woman makes more than the man does and in most cases the man is not working at all or he Is working and he owes back child support and out of a month's pay he is only bringing home $1,200.00 to $1,500.00 and he instantly feels no need to work or to just go back to the block, cop a pound break it down and sell drugs again or do some robberies. This pressure can affect a man in many ways, making him feel less of man or not a man at all, if you are in this situation as a woman, the worst thing you can do is throw these things in his face or treat him as if he isn't a man, instead support and encourage him to get going and possibly return to school so that he can get a better job… Remember, beside every great man, is a great woman that offered support when the man was down, offered love when he felt un-loved, offered her last dollar when he was broke… Money should never determine the size of your love for your spouse, because he bible says for richer or poorer, so there will be some poor days ahead and you must still stand strong together even at the lowest point in your marriage or at the point of losing it all because love covers all and withstands all.

2.) **Not being able to see his child by another woman.** This can cause so much hurt and pain and in most cases, he is not allowed to see the child based on the relationship he is currently in because the mother of the child is carrying spirits of jealousy, bitterness and envy. She will stop at nothing to ensure that his life is hell and he feels nothing but pain and if this isn't rectified, he will never feel like a man and he will always feel incomplete.

3.) **Having a felony and not given the opportunity to start over in life nor getting the job he desires because he has a felony.**

4.) <u>**Losing great friends because he's getting married.**</u> Sadly, this happens often and this hurts the man more than the woman will ever know, because she still has all her girls and they go out every so often and he has no one to go out with or talk to because he has made you his whole life. Truth is, every man needs is Primal time…

5.) <u>**Trying to take care of his mother.**</u>

6.) <u>**Not really having a father.**</u>

7.) <u>**Being molested.**</u> Yes, men are molested and some were even molested as little boys and this has carried over into their adulthood and now over into your marriage. This is why they have a lustful spirit that pulls their spirit to porn and no amount of porn can satisfy them because the more porn they watch the more spirits they're attracting to them. This can only be fixed through the power of Jesus and spiritual counseling with someone they trust.

8.) **<u>Lost faith in the church/pastor</u>**
9.) **<u>Feeling the streets is the only love you have...</u>**

There is so much that can be added to this list because the pain a man feels runs deeper and stretches farther than the ocean...

Men, please watch very closely over the spirits/things/people that you allow influencing your minds as the world makes it so easy to sin and you not even know it because once these things get into your mind can be used to destroy you and your marriage...

And a deceiving heart (Jeremiah 17:9) will take advantage of any situation to exploit it for sinful pleasures. We must watch against all this, and give ourselves to constant alertness against anything that would draw us away from the love of God and dividing our homes causing our marriages to fail.

Drive us away from our marriage, away from our children, away from our loved ones and those things that will drive us away from God... These things hidden deep with-in the man breaks down everything he touches, starting with the woman he loves most "his wife" and if he is hurting his wife, just imagine the pain that he is feeling because to cause her pain is to inflect pain on him-self...

How will we then as men, be spiritual, loving husbands, loving fathers, God fearing men, if we do not even know our own spirit, our own character, the way we operate, and the way we function, not knowing how important we are to God?

Men, find out the spirit of your soul, address the demons that are attacking you daily. Put down the toys and get in the game for God... God is calling you higher as a man and he requires so much more of you than what you are giving...

Never let anyone control your marriage, not even your mother. The bible says to let no one come between what God has put together and that no one includes you and the fleshly thoughts the devil might place on you to fall between the legs of another woman...

When you feel alone, talk to God! When you feel hurt, talk to God! When you feel less of man, talk to God to build you up! Talk to God to heal your past hurt and pain to get to know the real you and become the man God has called you to be...

Chapter 4

Luke 8:43-48
"Woman of God whatever issues hinder you? It's over"

So many women across the world, try to travel from relationship to relationship holding on to baggage from the last trip they were on and never empty/clean out the bag to prepare for the next trip and they can never take what God has for them to take on the trip because there is no room left in the bag, because of the things she's been carrying around for the last 18 years of traveling...
Women have been through/dealt with so many things in their lives from being molested, raped, beat, drugged, breast cancer, single parenting, child abuse, some molested by their fathers, uncles, brothers and in some cases even their friends and no one believed them when they tried to speak up thus leaving them with spirits of loneliness, depression, anger, hopelessness and fear that they will never find a man to love them despite the issues she has been through. While she has been set free from some of the issues in her life but, let us understand that most of the pain she will never tell her husband about in fear of how he may feel about her and she'll just suppress those things deep down inside of her telling herself that she has been delivered, when all the time she has not been fully healed/delivered and not being delivered from the hurt of your past can cause you to destroy every relationship you touch or get into...

"A Prayer to break those issues/things which hold you!!!"

God has written this book, so that whatever issues you have holding you or that you are holding onto, I claim right now in the name of Jesus that you are loosed from those issues right now as you read this book so that you can/will have a healthy marriage, that you get your life back in the name of Jesus, that every chain of hurt is removed from your life, every chain of being molested is broken in your life, that every chain of rape is broken in your life, that every chain of child abuse is broken in your life, every chain of being mentally broken is destroyed in your life, every chain of hopelessness is broken in your life, every chain of spiritual hurt is broken in your life, every chain of being sexually abused is broken in your life, every chain of bad marriages in your family is broken in your life, every chain that has been holding you down for the last 10 to 20 years be destroyed right now in the mighty name of Jesus, loosed that woman right now, demon you've got to go in the name Jesus, free her mind, free her soul, free her body, give back her life in the name of Jesus, give back her joy, give back her peace, give back her love, give back her happiness right now in the name of Jesus, you are free AMEN!!!!

It's time that you come out of that corner that you have been in hiding your past issues that are NOW in your present, that pain that still has you wounded like a gunned down animal, bleeding to death, that hurt, that has your mind fighting against your flesh. That hurt, that makes you wake up in cold sweats clenching your fist ready to fight… That hurt, that has you going to bed tired and waking up tired… That hurt that is causing cancer to rise up inside of you… That hurt, that has your internal organs fighting against each other. That hurt that keeps you confused, angry, bitter, alienated, unsure, insecure, un-happy, depressed, stressed, skeptical of everyone's love for you… That hurt, that has you going to bed crying, crying in your sleep, waking up crying, that hurt, that makes you question God and the plans he has for your life and asking God, "Why me!!!???" God says, "Why not you, aren't you strong enough, is not my grace sufficient enough to bring you out of this? Why do you not trust me, why won't you let go of the pain that is hurting you?"

"***Will you forever be the victim???***"
You need to stand firm at this very moment and yell to the top of your lungs.
"NO I WON'T!!!!" "MY BETTER ME STARTS RIGHT NOW!!!!"

Like this woman with the issue of blood she was forbidden from touching the priest because she was unclean… You've been suffering from this hurt for years, bleeding on the inside from this hurt for years… Feeling alienated because of this past hurt, but yet you stay determined because you know in order to move on with your life and have a great marriage, you must be determined to leave the past behind and reach to those things which are before you and be healed from it all…
Be healed:
    1.) From Rap!!!!
    2.) From Depression!!!
    3.) From Anger!!!
    4.) From Stress!!!

5.) From molestation!!!
6.) From prostitution!!!
7.) From child abuse!!!
8.) From Lust!!!
9.) From fortification!!!

- **If you don't get your healing:**

You will start to feel like everything that you touch is destroyed, everyone you've tried to love, every friendship and every man/woman, and all that you have ever loved has turned bad... Like the woman with the issue of blood, everything you touch while you are unclean will be destroyed because you haven't addressed the issues in your past and asked/allowed God to clean you making you whiter than snow... You can no longer hide behind the face paint that you call makeup that's burning your face and soul like hot coils piercing/melting everything that it even gets close to...
You must seek out the evil spirits that are upon you and remove them from you so that you can have a healthy life, marriage and soul, but doing this must first admit that you are not ok and there are some things or people in your past that have hurt you and tried to destroy you and you must forgive those who have done you wrong or the person that you are trying to marry will become the victim and you'll never be able to trust him/her, truly love him/her and in most cases the marriage will end up in destruction because those unclean things that you are holding to will cause the marriage to be destroyed...
I have listed some spiritual characteristics that can help you to look deep within yourself to see if any of these spirits are upon you...
We'll start with asking a few questions to do some self searching:
Answer these un-forgiveness questions honestly:

1) I find myself holding grudges.
2) I retreat into isolation from others.
3) I erupt in anger or I boil inside.
4) I think of ways to get even with others who hurt me.
5) I just bury the wrongs done to me without really addressing them.
6) I pity myself.
7) I carry bitterness and anger towards those who have hindered me or willfully, purposely wronged me.
8) Instead of stating the truth, I make excuses for those who wronged or hurt me.
9) I often feel sorry for myself.
10) Occasionally I think of killing myself for what someone has done to me.
11) Nobody has had it as bad as me.
12) I want to get even with people who've caused me pain. 13) I insulate or protect myself behind the walls of defensiveness.
14) I don't trust others.
15) I just can't forgive.

16) I'm angry with God for allowing bad things to happen to me.
17) I act like nothing happen instead of confronting issues that have hurt me.
18) I can't get over my past.
19.) I am insecure because of my past.
20.) My past hurt makes it hard for me to love myself.
If you have 5 – 9 "Yes's", you're in the [50%] of operating in a spirit of un-forgiveness.

If you have 10 – 14 "Yes's", you're in the [75%] of operating in a spirit of un-forgiveness. You're in bondage, un-happy, bitter and sinking into depression.

Marriage of Pearls

If you have 15 or "Yes's", you are operating with a stronghold of unforgiveness. This stronghold has to be broken from your life immediately and you must remove the demons holding it in place in your life, causing you to have a destructive life style with no one wanting to be around you.

Angry Destroys the Peace
Anger Destroys the Joy
Anger Destroys the Patience
Anger Destroys the Self-control
Anger Destroys the Love
Anger Destroys the Goodness
Anger Destroys the Gentleness
Anger Destroys the Self Respect
Anger Destroys the Dignity and Honor
Anger Destroys the Balance and Stability
Anger Destroys the Material Things of Value (By throwing, Smashing, Banging and Breaking)
Anger Destroys the Moral and Social Values
Anger Destroys the Righteousness
Anger Destroys the Wisdom
Anger Destroys the Discretion and Judgment
Anger Destroys the Spiritual Growth
Anger Destroys the emotional and spiritual Strength
>   The end result is the Anger will destroy your marriage!!!
>   When a person gets angry that person maybe physically,
>   biologically and chemically affected in a variety of ways thus
>   causing strain in/on the marriage/relationship and will act in
>   the manner listed below:

Generating Heat
Steaming
Smoking
Secreting Acid

Boiling
Burning on the inside
Palpitation of the heart
Getting Exhausted
Perspiring
Getting High Blood Pressure
Heart Attack
Stroke

Anger is a Curse - Genesis 49:7: This scripture tells us that anger is a curse and the reason why it should never be brought into a marriage because you curse your marriage when the spirit of anger is present.

Leaving your spouse feeling broken and destroyed...

Marriage of Pearls

Poem written by Pastor DuJuan S Boyd

The Broken Spouse....
Are you in love with your spouse?
Can you hear his/her silent screams for help?
Or do you just have him/her enslaved in a trap like mouse
That fell in love with the wrong cheese?
They cry themselves to sleep
Begging God please
Please hear my cry
Please heal my pain
Please God tell my why!!!!!???
Why do I feel this hurt, this pain that cuts through my soul
so deep???
So deep it's hard for me to even sigh
Sometimes I just want to clock out and tell the whole world
bye
Because I feel like I have nothing else to gain
This pressure I feel is about to drive me insane
I do my best to be a great spouse
But God I am tired of my spouse manipulating my brain
Treating me like trash
Only nice when it's time to make love
God I am so hurt and destroyed that I am not in the mood

And besides, I don't even feel safe with the glove.
Lord I can only talk to you
Because, you know what I have been through
And no one understands like you...
The hurt, the pain, the rape, the shame, the beat, the blood,
the stress, no love
I used to believe my spouse was a gift from heaven above
But that's not true
Because you would never send me a person this evil
God, I just want my relationship back with you.
Make me new and fill me with more of you
Remove the stress, pain, drama and fear
Through this pain I feel, I know you are near
At times I feel my spouse doesn't even care!!!
Please God remove me from the wild
Please count/remember my tears
And clean the evil in my house
Signed your child...
The broken spouse....

- **<u>"Don't marry HIM until you touch the HEM!!!!!"</u>**

Chapter 5

Revelations 17:4

Never corrupt the covenant!!!

The woman wore purple clothes, bright red clothes, gold jewelry, gems, and pearls. In her hand she was holding a gold cup filled with detestable and evil things from her sexual sins.

When entering into a marriage you want to ensure that you are committed to that marriage/person understanding that you are making a covenant between you and God when you say I DO on your special day with your soul mate.

That I DO is really a direct promise to God that you will not allow anyone to break or come between what God has put together...

Covenant- A covenant (Hebrew berith, Greek diatheke) is a legal agreement between two or more parties. The word "covenant(s)" occurs 284 times in the Old Testament (as found in the New American Standard Bible). "Covenant(s)" occurs 37 times in the New Testament, which gives a total of 321 occurrences.

Using covenants is how God communicates to us, how God redeems us, and guarantees us eternal life for our souls. A covenant is a promise, and God's promises cannot be broken since they rest in his infinite, pure character.

Let's look at some ways the covenant can be corrupted:
1. **Sex outside marriage:** It does not matter if you are un-happy, not being satisfied at home, drunk, high, marriage is falling apart, separated or whatever the case maybe, a covenant is made.

1 Corinthians 6:16 "What? Know ye not that he which is joined to an harlot is one body? For two, saith he, shall be one flesh" so, you are no longer 2 but are now 1 flesh, 1 body and 1 soul. During sex today with someone other than your spouse many things are transferred, diseases, body fluid, and liquid. Spiritually, a lot of transaction take place, a person you might sleep with outside of you marriage will have many demons, let's say 1,000 demons, this person now slept with a clean person that used to be you, you will collect 500 demons from this person. Again, with 500 demons you are now sexually loose, you start to sleep with another person, and the new girl/man will get 250 out of the 500. It goes on and on. The life of this man/girl is divided, shared, anytime he does it, he can never remain the same.

Also, the first time you had sexual intercourse and the way it was done, has a heavy spiritual consequence tide to it in the spirit.

2. If you have promised to marry somebody and you change your mind about that person, and in 1 hand you love them but in the other hand you're holding a former boyfriend/ girlfriend can become a very powerful tool of the devil to charge his demon filled spirits to enter your relationship and your mind causing you to enter into demonic covenants not only with these unclean spirits but with the person you're seeking to marry or are already married to.

3. **Blood Covenants:** Every incision made, every cut in the body, every mark in the body, are all covenants with these spirits. You have Lovers' cutting each other, mixing the blood with the wine to drink is a destructive covenant. In a marriage, your blood belongs to your spouse and no one else as God created you both to be one, that you are to be bonded as one… Any blood covenant is the very powerful because life is in the blood as we were saved by the blood of Jesus and without the blood we're not saved, our sins are not forgiven, our iniquity still stands…

4. **Counterfeit Love/Lust:** The devil has corrupted so many

Marriage of Pearls

covenants/marriages, he has created a counterfeit person of your spouse, a person who looks, like, talks like, walks like, smells, like, dresses like and everything else that is in your spouse that you love and he's also added things that attracts you In a lustful way is in that person and the thing/things you are missing in your spouse is what you attach yourself to and you will fall into corrupting your marriage. Whenever there is an original, there must be counterfeit, the original will always have something the counterfeit doesn't have and in this case it is what God has used to connect you and your spouse and that is the soul, the soul of your spouse can never be duplicated and whatever you find in the counterfeit person "false love" will only satisfy you for so long and just like any counterfeit, it is only accepted by those who feel that they can't do/get anything better in life, so they lower their standards and purchase the knock off but in this case purchasing the knock off will cost you more than money, it will cost you your soul in the end…

Never trade in the original for a knockoff!!! It will never produce the same quality and the souls are not built the same and will never connect with you on the level God has you connected to the person you are about to marry or are already married to… The saying is 80/20 when you step outside of your marriage but when it deals with a God fearing person that you are cheating and committing sin against, you are not even getting 1% from the other person, the only gain you will get is the gain of lustful sin, leading to death once the sin is finished…

5. **Occultism covenant:** Cult society, they swear allegiance promising they will never leave the group with blood. This person will offer you the world and everything in it and they don't have any means to even provide for themselves… They will look good in outer appearance and are all trashed, dirty, filled with viruses and sleeping unclean spirits that are just waiting to destroy you and once you have been destroyed and your blood has been spilled, they walk away leaving you in the midst of your destruction will the walls of your life falling down all around you and you now have no one to turn to but God himself because you have broken/corrupted your covenant that was your marriage…

6. **Food and drinks:** Food collected from the agent of darkness. Beware; food can kill especially free food. Some are initiated into the demonic realms of life through food. The main food here is lust as lust carries a multitude of spiritual foods that can kill you… Lust is very selfish, to the point of death to the one he seeks to satisfy him and when his satisfaction is not met, "LUST" becomes very anger, violent, manipulative, bitter and the imagination of this spirit will bring other spirits of destruction such as Leviathan or Python and this spirit will stop at nothing to break you or your marriage down to get what it seeks to be satisfied.
James 1:15. "Then when lust hath conceived, it bringeth forth sin: and sin, when it is finished, bringeth forth death."

Marriage of Pearls

So bringing lust into your marriage kills it from the very start, even if you only lusted in your mind after someone other than your spouse and that is why porn is such a demonic destroyer of marriages because you have men and women lusting after other men and women and those spirits attach themselves to the person watching and causing them to watch porn more than they have sex with their spouse and in some cases the spouse isn't even attractive to them anymore and the spouse begins to feel un-wanted, alone, in-sexy, cheated on, and in most cases, start to try and figure what they're doing wrong to be un-wanted by their spouse.

The first stage of sin is lust, which can be described as those long looks at someone else, double-takes as the man/woman walks by you, rubbing on the neck or shoulders of someone other than your spouse, and undressing a man/woman is in your path of vision.

Women/Men are three-dimensional creatures with spirits, souls and bodies, with relationships, responsibilities and dreams for their lives. When we lust, we remove all these aspects God has placed in that person and just look at their outer being/bodies, legs, lips, face, butt, and chest and even make the way they look at us inviting. We objectify into things, instead of souls created by God. In lust, we devalue the amazing soul that a woman/man is and make her/him into a lust hit thoughts on a playground in our brains.

The second stage of the seed of lust is sin. The sin in most cases starts very off small, like inappropriate humor, jokes, asking about a woman's/man's marriage, asking if they happy, looking for a hole to seek into or telling her/him how bad your marriage is, planting seeds of displeasure in the household, pointing all the wrong things in the marriage and promising that you will never do the things If he/she was with you, a hug, a longer hug, an even longer hub, private meetings and then kissing, sex and lunch sex. Sin is the evidence that you have fertilized lust over a period of time. Since sin is the next growth stage of lust, it doesn't just happen; there is always a process of nurturing the seed of lust in your mind…

Of course the last stage of lust is death!!!!

7. **<u>Demonic fashion</u>**: Wearing clothes that expose your body/flesh will give demons access to your body and will draw men/women with like-minded sprits to you, only for the open flesh that they see and in most cases, this is why people today keep drawing in different men/women but they all have the same spirits and they're only after one thing, the **"FLESH"** they see. Fashion has been proven to be affective in how people see you, what people buy, how companies sell you on watching even a T.V. show and how people respond to you/treat you and it is important that you're in the marriage season with the proper attire of marriage on, even after marriage, it is important that you keep the proper attire on for marriage... We'll dig more into that in the next few chapters...

You'll know that evil spirits have corrupted your marriage/covenant because they will be resistant to the word of God, going to church, reading the bible or even praying with you and in some cases they will try and talk you out of your religion. talk about the church you attend, tell you that you are spending too much time at/with the church and even tell you that you don't need church, let's just go back to the way we or you used to be, we were happier then but In reality you were all but happy in your old life of sin... Not everyone will join in on the merriment of your happiness and new found joy in the lord and they will do whatever they can to drag you back into the hell you just came out of, but don't you give in, don't you turnaround and don't look back, keep your eyes focused on what God has placed in-front of you... Don't even entertain those spirits anymore, there is a reason you no longer feel comfortable around certain people and their spirits and that is because God has healed you and called you out from among them but you still want to have get together and invite them just to keep fitting in with them, to feel accepted and not rejected.

Some will even try to start arguments with you about your new walk, but just because you're invited to an argument doesn't mean that you have to attend it and give them the pleasure of tossing their sprits all

Marriage of Pearls

in your atmosphere, trying to destroy what you have and steal your joy that inside you.

The flesh will tell your mind that you want this man/woman but it will never tell you that this could not only destroy your marriage, it will also destroy your soul, leaving you left with nothing in life and leaving you falling to hell in the afterlife. Always appreciate what you have regardless of the issues that your marriage may face, never step outside of your marriage, be faithful, work things out, pray about these things and let God move in every area of your marriage…

Chapter 6

Forgiveness Before Getting Married

Truly forgiving she/he is the only way to set yourself free from the bondage/stronghold of the evil spirits and hurt that is draining you. The resentment, bitterness, and sometimes pure rage will slowly kill you on the inside and you will never be truly happy. They will manifest in emotional and physical illness, constricting your life so that you are little more than the sum of my grievances and pains.

At many points I am sure your emotions have consumed you and at times it even hurts you to smile in the face of his family, bit by bit, until there is nothing but the memory of your overwhelming, righteous fury.

It will take you years to forgive, but you must do your part to transform this relationship because and decide that it was worth saving, but it won't always be easy.

There will be/have been times when you've gotten caught up in painful memories instead of being present in the relationship setting an atmosphere of draining spirits. Destroying more of you and more of this relationship as I am sure he feels the pressure.

If you choose not to for whatever reason, if you feel that this is worth fighting for, these ideas may help you stay—and stay happy—in this relationship as it is:

1. Realize that you can't make someone change (if they don't want to).

Marriage of Pearls

If they aren't open to that, you can only change how you respond and relate to them."His/her Family will always want to control the relationship and in most cases places you in a bad place in the family because the old girlfriend/boyfriend is still coming around the family and being treated as family" Knowing this, you may decide that you're not able to maintain this relationship. You need to be honest with yourself here: is it really healthy to stay in this situation?

Create space to heal and then rebuilt a new, healthier relationship after the dynamics have transformed.

2. Determine what you need.

You may feel that you can only forgive if this person fully acknowledges everything that hurt you and then takes responsibility for all of it. You may need to go to seek biblical counseling, either alone or with him. Or it may be sufficient for you to recognize remorse in actions and then work, on your own, to release your feelings.

You are allowed to need whatever you need—but it's crucial that you identify it. If you know you can't move on with the marriage or even the relationship until you receive a thorough confession and apology, but that just isn't happening, you will set yourself up for more pain and unhappiness, finding yourself depressed in your sleep, trying to find a way out of the marriage you've gotten yourself into.

3. After your needs are met, do the work to forgive.

Theirs is a quote written by David L. Kuper PhD: "Forgiveness is giving up all hope of a better past." That's what it truly means to really forgive someone that has wronged you in anyway: accept/deal with what happened, choose to find at least some understanding for the other person's actions in being un-faithful and hurtful towards you, and then decide it's in your best interest to let it go and move on. You can let the relationship go and move on or you can decide that the relationship Is worth fixing and move on.

Forgiving is something we may need to do repeatedly and in most cases daily because there will be people that do us wrong daily and we are not to harbor those feelings inside of us and just like Jesus on the cross who asked God to forgive them for they know not what they do, we are to do the same. What's important is that you NEED/DESIRE to forgive—that you're heart and soul is open and willing to have compassion for that person and see them without the sunglasses of hurt on, even if it isn't always easy.

If you don't feel like you can do that, for whatever reason, you may need to take time and then come back to it at a later date. It's far better to take space and then to reconnect when you're ready to forgive than it is to preserve a relationship that just gets more depression, stressed and hopelessness with each passing day.

4. Assess your boundaries.

It's a lot easier to forgive someone for a mistake or series of mistakes if you set clear boundaries for the relationship going forward.

You need to ask yourself if something needs to change in order for you to feel safe and happy in the relationship as it is. Do you need to spend less time together? Do you need to be clear that certain topics are not open for discussion? Do you need to assert yourself when the other person starts talking to you in a certain way?

If you suspect that someone may physically harm you, I strongly suggest you consult a professional who is trained to assist with domestic violence cases. This is a far different situation, as one slip-up could cost your life.

5. Practice mindfulness.

This is the most difficult part for some: every so often when you're interacting with this person, memories from years ago resurface—memories you've released many times before. Generally, the present moment looks nothing like the past, but a word or a look can sometimes remind you how angry you felt back then.

I suspect this may be inevitable in situations like this. Over time the memories become far less frequent, but they always have the potential to

Marriage of Pearls

pop back up because we are only human. Still, we are far more than the sum of our emotions and reactions.

We don't need to let ourselves get swept away in anger, disappointment, or anything else that hurts. This doesn't mean we won't feel these things. In fact, it's a good thing that we do. If we didn't feel our pains, we likely wouldn't feel our joys.

It means we can identify our emotions, sit with them, and then choose to challenge the thoughts that might exacerbate them.

The alternative is to rehash the past in your head—going through everything you wish didn't happen, how you feel about the fact that it did, what you wish you did or said then, and how much you hope nothing similar ever happens again. It's a lot easier to be present when you breathe through your feelings than it is when you obsess about them.

6. Open up to joy!

If you've chosen to maintain this relationship, you must feel that there's something in it for (both of) you, or else you wouldn't do it. Take the time to enjoy each other, living mindfully in the present, within the new boundaries you've set.

If you spend the majority of your time rehashing old stories or making this person repeatedly earn your forgiveness, this relationship won't have a life in the present—it will just be a shadow of the past. And what's the point of holding onto that? It would be far kinder to just set this person free than to stay connected by a pain you refuse to release.

Relationships aren't easy. People make mistakes, but even the deepest wounds can heal and the most strained relationships can transform. We just need to learn to recognize when it's healthy to hold on and when it's wiser to let go.

Only you know what's right for you in this moment, and only you can find the courage to honor it.

Forgiveness is essential to a marriage as there will be mistakes made and fights over things that will at times feel/seem like it is the end of the marriage, but if we can't learn to forgive in the marriage and move forward then the marriage is already set for destruction from the start of it.

Forgiveness starts with self and learning to forgive yourself in all that you have done to others, learning to let things go that have happened to you because as long as you hold on to the things that have happened to you then there is no way that you can have anything healthy in life, a marriage or any relationship because you will always have thoughts of what someone has done to you in the past and the past will always outweigh your current love and you will never be able to fully trust in any relationship/marriage as long as you have things from your past that you haven't dealt with.

Chapter 7

"Scriptures & Prayers for Your Marriage"

The following are Scriptures and prayers that can be used to pray for your marriage. These prayers are based on the Word of God and the power of the Holy Spirit I have blessed them with. Plead them with confidence and with faith that God will repair your marriage.

God, I Declare and Decree that we will speak the truth in love to each other, honestly and openly sharing our deepest feelings with each other, supporting each other, never trying to hurt each other but always holding one another up in the name of Jesus Amen. (Ephesians 4:15, 25).

Lord, I pray that our marriage will glorify you and be an example to others through our love, we promise to let to show your intention for what true love in marriage really is (1 Corinthians 10:31).

God, I plead that you would give us wisdom and compassion in dealing with our in-laws and that you would not allow them to come between what you have put together. God please allow my spouse to be released from their mother, because at times I feel as if I am in competition with the parents of my spouse and they always seem to come before me and at times God, I feel as if I am not accepted into their family and always end up feeling left out, alone, alienated and I can feel them talking about me when I leave the room. God I am asking for peace and protection in this area of our marriage because I know that it can destroy us if it is not fixed by you, so please touch everyone's heart that is a part of our families so that we can all grow as a big happy family, loving each other and supporting each other, in the name of Jesus Amen. (Matthew 5:7).

God, please, bless and strengthen our marriage right now in the midst of the pressures and trials of our lives as we are going through problems that are affecting this marriage, our finances are low, we are not able to buy food, my spouse has lost their job and life seems so hard right now and the more we need the more we seem distant from each other and I know this should bring us closer to each other but it's hard with all this over our heads and we just don't know what else to do God and we are turning to asking that you please turn it all around for us as you have done it before, please God fix our finances in the name of Jesus, show us favor, bring us out of the lion's den God, for they are trying to devour us at every corner with no mercy they roar at us while scratching their claws against the dry dirt in which we stand, positioned and ready to attack, so please God step in right now and save us, this marriage and our family in the name of Jesus Amen. (2 Corinthians 12:9).

Father, I ask you to protect our marriage from the attacks of Satan. Deliver us from his evil, destructive plans that he put in place to destroy our marriage, God please raise up a standing against these enemies that trying to come against us like a flood and be a fence around us every day, getting the wild life out of our yard of love in this marriage and we promise we will give your name the praise in Jesus name Amen. (1 Peter 5:8).

Father, grant that we might find great delight and joy in each , that we may find ways to keep our passion for each other burning and if for some reason the flames go out, we find our first love in each other and stir up what is beneath the ashes just waiting to receive fresh air to re-spark the flame in us, but most of all God, please be our fluid, lighter, guider and savior in our marriage so that we may have you as the head of it all and as you lead we shall follow and for peace in you, where our true joy lies. (Proverbs 5:18).

Lord God, I pray that you would deepen and strengthen our friendship to each other, let us be able to talk to each other about what is troubling us, allow us to laugh together, pray together and always do things as one. (Proverbs 17:17).

Marriage of Pearls

Father, I ask that your power would sustain and give stability to this marriage (Jeremiah 32:17).

Father, help us to discern and deal with those things and people that hinder and hurt our relationship not only in our marriage but those vices and people that hinder our relationship with you father God. (Psalm 139:23-24).

God, I ask that our strengths would overcome our weaknesses (Genesis 2:20-23).

I pray that we would be kind and tenderhearted to one another, forgiving one another even as Christ's has forgiven us, let us hold no bitterness, no anger, no envy or any ill feelings toward each other and once we forgive for what has been done, I ask that you help to never bring it up ever again. (Ephesians 4:32).

I plead that we would be sensitive to the needs and hurts of each other. Enable us to minister to each other in these areas (Matthew 20:28).

God, create within us a hunger for each other. Let us be satisfied with one another so that no one can offer anything that can cause lust to come into our marriage, let us thirst for each other daily and give us the strength to keep our minds set on you, so that we can always have our hearts set on each other in Jesus name Amen. (Proverbs 5:19-20).

I plead that you would give us a heart to seek after you and serve you all the days of our lives (Psalm 63:1).

Father, I pray that you would grant us the wisdom and power to gain and use our finances wisely (Proverbs 3:9-10).

Lord, I ask that you would deliver us from pettiness and un forgiveness in our relationship because it seems that no matter how many times I apologize, it seems that I am never really forgiven because it is always thrown in my face and I am really hating this marriage because of it, yes I still love my spouse, but I hate their ways and how I am always thrown to the wolves because of my past faults in this relationship, so please God see fit to touch my spouse's heart so that I am truly forgiven and so that we can officially try to move forward and save our marriage. (Matthew 18:20-21).

Father, I plead that we will surrender all that we are and all that we have to each other (Genesis 2:24-25).

I pray that we would love you with all our being and our neighbors as ourselves (Matthew 22:37-40).

Lord God, I ask that we would love and obey Your Word, building our lives, marriage, and family on its truth. (Psalm 119:97).

Father, I plead that we would be patient with each other in all the circumstances of life (1 Corinthians 13:4).

Father, I pray that we will be kind and gentle to each other through the ups and downs of our life together (1 Corinthians 13:4).   Father, I ask that we would not let any jealousy or envy gain ground in our relationship (1 Corinthians 13:4).

God, I plead that we will always seek what is best for our relationship (1 Corinthians 13:5).

Lord, I pray that we will share each other's burdens and hurts (1 Corinthians 13:5).

Father, enable us to overcome the pride in our lives. Set us free from the pride that will hinder and hurt our marriage (1 Corinthians 13:5).

Lord, I ask that we would not be rude or thoughtless concerning each other (1 Corinthians 13:5).

God, deliver us from the selfishness that would hinder and hurt our relationship (1 Corinthians 13:5).

Lord, I ask that we would rejoice in each other's strengths and gifts and would pray concerning our weaknesses and sins (1 Corinthians 13:6).

Marriage of Pearls

Father, I pray that You would give us a love that bears all things, believes all things, and hopes all things (1 Corinthians 13:7).

Lord, I plead that You would create in us a love that will endure the stress and problems that we will face (1 Corinthians 13:7).

Father, I ask that our love for one another will never fail (1 Corinthians 13:8).

Father, I plead that we would be faithful to attend and serve in the church of Jesus Christ (Hebrews 10:25).

Praying together brings couples into agreement as we petition God and thank Him for our blessings.

Praying together is vital to a lasting marriage.

Keeping God at the center of your marriage sustains the covenant between you.

Trust the Lord to help you build a healthy marriage with a harmony that goes beyond anything you can imagine without Him. Our partnered prayers result in the following:

It develops a deeper ability for communication. This is fundamental to a real and long-lasting companionship.

It provides the way to a humble heart. As we humble ourselves in prayer we are also humbled before our spouses, keeping us open, honest and sincere. This brings us into a closer intimacy with each other and strengthens mutual respect.

Our marriage will build accountability as we pray together 'for our marriage' and the problems that arise. He will show us the solutions for working things out. By submitting ourselves to each other, we develop a deeper trust in our spouses and in the Lord (Ephesians 5:21-26).

Nothing can be more valuable in the lives of children than the united prayers of their parents. In Matthew 18:19-20 Jesus says "…If two of you agree here on earth concerning anything you ask, my Father in heaven will do it for you. For where two or three gather together because they are mine, I am there among them."

Hebrews 13:4 says "Give honor to marriage, and remain faithful to one another in marriage…" Pray together, and for each other, that you each remain faithful and enjoy the goodness of marriage. Romance is important (read the Song of Solomon together), commitment is vital; honesty is essential and prayer to the Lord necessary. Remember the words of this prayer when you go together before Him

- **A Prayer against Adultery.**

God, I come to you right now in the mighty name of Jesus, asking that you raise up a hedge of thorns around my marriage and my spouse God. So that whoever is lusting after my spouse or who my spouse has lusted for, that they lose interest right now in the mighty name of Jesus God. Please allow my spouses mind to be loosed from this spirit God and return to me in this marriage and force every lusting spirit/person out of our lives right now in the mighty name of Jesus, I claim it to be so, Amen.

- **Prayer against Pornography in a marriage.**

PRAYER AGAINST THE DEMON OF PORNOGRAPHY, DESTROYING MARRIAGES!

Father, we thank you for the power of your holy word, that is our weapon with which we are empowered and authorized to pull down every strong hold erected against marriage.

Right now, we the men and women of faith, uncover the hidden and deadly trick of the enemy and we come against the foul and perverted spirit of pornography that is tearing Godly marriages apart.

We strangulate the immoral desire of self-pleasure that is affecting husbands and wives alike. We come against the desires to indulge in pornographic movies, books, magazines, explicit images and every strategically positioned diversion from wholesome romance in marriage.

We come against the providers of pornography. Every adult film maker, every adult book store, every internet site and even the strip clubs. We bind up the desire of both husband and wives from wasting the family finances on this filth. We speak a halt to all the time spent on pornography, which could be QUALITY time spent with each other in wholesome love.

To every young man and woman whose spouse is not enough for them, because they have been satisfying their flesh before marriage with pornography, we claim deliverance and the freedom to love in a Godly manner, in Jesus' name.

We declare and decree that this vile and repugnant infiltration and attack on God ordained marriages is over in the mighty name of Jesus. Amen!

Hebrews 13:4 Let marriage be held in honor among all, and let the marriage bed be undefiled, for God will judge the sexually immoral and adulterous

- **Prayer for Sexual Healing after abuse.**

First, before we get to the prayer, let us understand that when we misuse our sexuality through any form of sin we give Satan permission to attack us in our sexuality, thus attacking our marriage. A man/woman who engages in pornography of any kind will always be found in a deep struggle, trying to resist lust in a marriage, even resisting simply looking at the breast of the waitress that is serving you and in most cases making your spouse feel insecure, not pretty to you any more, unworthy, depressed trying to figure out what she is doing wrong and why are you looking at this filth and she is right in the other room. Have I gained too much weight? Is he tired of me?

Or for the woman, lusting after that fine man with the rock hard AB's you seen on T.V. A woman who is sexually promiscuous before marriage will always at times find herself wrestling with temptations many years afterwards because in most cases she's remained friends with the very person she was lusting for.

That is why it is so important to bring your sexuality under the protection of our lord and savior Jesus Christ and seek his cleansing for all our sexual sins we may have committed, rather it be before or after we said I DO.

Second, Sexual abuse/brokenness, whether it was through abuse as a child or just abuse through our own actions or actions of others, it can/will create sexual difficulties in a marriage/relationship and will always leave an open gateway for the enemy to enter our marriage to destroy it. Forgiveness is always a must to heal us from our sexual abuse so that we can be healed and have a healthy marriage, but we must have both the confidence that we have truly forgiven those that have oppressed us in a sexual way and that we are truly forgiven by God for the sexual sins we have committed and in the end our marriage will prove to be immensely freeing until death do us part. God I ask that you deliver me and my spouse from our sexual sins that we have committed and brought into our marriage. God please release me from the pornography in the name of Jesus, make my mind to not lust for that mess anymore Jesus, I need to be cleansed from it all God, as I am destroying my marriage every time I do it. Each time I have ejaculated from these lust God, please don't kill for this sin I have committed God; I need you to deliver me right now God. Each time I have even thought of touching myself without my spouse present God, please forgive me, release from my past molestation so that I can move forward from this, because what I seek in this is a form of what has happened to me in the past and God you know my past hurt, please help me to forgive those that have taken my pearls, but I know that you can and will give them back more precious than ever in Jesus name I claim it to be so. Amen.

- **Prayer against strip clubs!**

God I come to your right now asking that you heal the mind of my spouse and whatever lustful things that are drawing my spouse into the strip club, please remove it right now in the name of Jesus!!! Allow me to be all that my spouse is in need of, mentally, physically and emotionally, God I really need you because these frequent trips are hindering our marriage and I am not sure how much I can take of this, so I ask that you deliver us right now from this spirit of lust God so that we can be healed, so that we can love again, so that we can become one again, so that we can praise your name for bringing us out and seeing fit to allow us to see you in our storms. I know that you are able and I know that you hear me, so God please have your way with my spouse, remove these thoughts and emotions from him, allow the strippers to not be attractive to him any longer as this is also hurting our finances and bills are not getting paid. God please, this is my final cry, HELP!!! In Jesus name AMEN!!!

- Prayer against spiritual church hurt in a marriage.

God I ask that you heal the mind, body and soul of our marriage God. The place where we have been worshipping or at least thought we were is driving a wedge between my spouse and I... God!!! I want to leave but my spouse desires to stay and I am pleading with you today, please heal me from this hurt I feel. Lord I go out of support for my spouse and my soul is not with me and through the broken smiles and the griped teeth I am hurt deep inside in fear of losing my spouse in order to save my soul and I know this not your will for us God. Please destroy whatever curse is on my spouse and I, please remove any false words that have been spoken over us right now in the name of Jesus, give us peace, give us our joy back in the midst of the storm with the wind blowing like a mighty rushing wind I feel tossed all around, beat up, step on and I am at the point where I can no longer get up, please hear me God, I need you more than ever right now, I need to know that you hear me, that you'll deliver us, that you'll make things right in your name, that you'll bring back the love that we once shared God... God your word said left no man put asunder what you have put together and God I feel in my spirit that this church is hurting us with its destructive ways God, so please help us and we promise to give your name all the praise, all the honor, in Jesus mighty name AMEN!!!

Chapter 8

Why Marriages Struggle/How to Overcome Them

1.) **Individual Pursuits (Selfishness).** This can become an issue in a marriage and an issue of balance in loving, caring, thoughtfulness and consideration. Because people will at times make things all about them in a marriage, even in arguments, they become the victim in any situation, when in reality both parties are the victim. The person can never see any wrong in what they do. They foster themselves in a corner when storms come when in fact they started the problem and come back to the relationship as if nothing ever happened, anger instantly turns to smiles and laughter, leaving the other spouse pondering if this person is really crazy or just needs help. Yes!!! They need help from themselves, everything can't be about you in a marriage, so what you don't like football, try watching a game with him just for some quality time. So what you don't enjoy shopping with her, go with her and learn what she really likes. My point is, we must do things in a marriage that we at times don't like to do and there must be give and take 100% across the board. No more playing the victim, no more mind games, no more searching through phones, emails, face book, twitter because you feel some kind of way. Forgive yourself for what you've done so that you can learn how to trust in a marriage, love in a marriage and be a vessel that can help your marriage and stop spreading your business all over the world... So what your spouse made a mistake, we all do,

keep that stuff in house and deal with it or leave it…
Individual pursuit will only destroy your marriage!!!!

2.) **Lack of commitment: loyalty, fidelity and devotion.**
Loyalty means everything in a marriage, everything to your spouse and without it, your marriage has nothing to stand on because how can you even have truth if you first don't have any loyalty in the marriage??? Easy answer! You can't!!! Support your spouse in every battle that comes, stand strong together and be mindful not to talk to others about your marriage in a way that can breach the trust that you two share with each other… The smallest things said can and at times will be twisted so that the person you talked can seem like they have some dirt to speak on regarding your marriage and those that do that only wish they had a life/marriage that they could talk about, so be careful of who you are talking to/with about your marriage… Fidelity means to be honest at all times, being contestant in your actions, doing this will build the trust foundation in your marriage. Never have a reason to lie and be disloyal to your spouse because all things can be talked about/worked out if approached the proper way. Let your spouse know through your action, that they can count on you even when the road is tough, no money is coming in and the whole world seem to be crashing down on you both. Pray with each other and watch God move mountains for your marriage… Devotion is your sacrifice, your energy, your time, what are you putting the marriage??? Are you giving all that you can? Even if you are, always try to give more and always put your marriage first in all things outside of God…

3.) **Lack of unity of purpose: understanding what you and your spouse want from a marriage**. Marriage is walked into so lightly now and is becoming just the next thing to do, something to say that we've done in life and there is never a clear vision for the marriage, the two never sit and come up with a plan, they just go with the flow of the marriage and they never really start building on anything strong because there was never a foundation to begin with. We must understand/have a clear understanding of the marriage we want/need and what we expect from the person we are married to, so that we can be clear in both words and actions from both parties. This will cause you to create clear boundaries and expectations in your marriage from the start and also help you and spouse communicate more clearly of your hopes, dreams and desires that you want/need out of your marriage so that it doesn't end up in divorce as many marriages are today. Set standards of what is accepted and what is not in your marriage but at the same time, giving each other that time alone if needed. This step can make or break your marriage at any given point or argument if things are not talked about to begin with how then can we expect talk about them once there is a disagreement and please whatever you do, never argue in front of the children because they will grow thinking that is how things In a marriage should be handled when it is the complete opposite.

4.) **Striving for reciprocity rather than mutuality.** There is a big difference in giving a compliment because you want to get one in return "selfish" and totally giving one because you truly mean it and you really want to make your spouse feel special. As a marriage goes on, there tends to be a sense of insecurities at times and we begin to want reassurance that you are still attractive to your spouse, so seek we these compliments as part of our reassurance in our marriage to lessen our insecurities and we become angry, hurt, feeling alone, bitter when our spouse doesn't reciprocity the way we think they should for our intentions. However, if you two are striving for a healthy marriage and God is centered in it and the base of it, those insecurities, regardless of how large they are will be dispelled-because your love for each other will always overcome all things that you face. So always strive for mutuality and not reciprocity so that both of you are pleased and happy. Complement each other often and have date night once a week at-least so that you can have a real reason to gaze at each other and complement each other without saying a word.

5.) **Not understanding the nature and dynamics of true intimacy.** When we hear the word intimacy, we instantly think of sexual things and miss the true meaning of this word. Most women get it and would rather have this true word in a marriage more than the actual sexual acts. This word literally refers to the openness or the emotional level thereof and the availability you provide your spouse. Always having girls night out or football night with the guys more than you are with your spouse can/will destroy your marriage in the long run… There must be some form of intimate sharing in a marriage, comfort, showing that you are willing to engage in… Because too often we expect complete openness, total disclosure with-holding nothing from each other and this is the way it is in when the relationship first starts but as the years go by, this becomes less and less to the point of dissatisfaction in the marriage and leading to a divorce. We must learn how to maintain a high level of intimacy in our marriages so that we can keep them strong and also understand there some things that your spouse is just not going to tell you to keep from hurting you or getting you all upset… I promise you wouldn't your spouse telling about person that hit on them at the store that day she/he went by themselves. This happens more to women than men, so let's face it, there are some things we are just not going to be told, live with that and have an open marriage. No way am I saying, sit up all night and gossip about your friends issues but focus more on the inner needs of your spouse, draw closer to each other, look deeply into each other's eyes in an attempt to see the soul of the other person and I promise you, that the connection you feel will connect you forever.

6.) **Not understanding the nature of real love.** We have to start off first, asking two questions "what is real love to you?" "Do you really love yourself?" Because before we can truly know what real love is, we must first be able to answer both of these questions and be 100% honest with ourselves when we do. How can we expect someone else to love us, when we don't even love ourselves, forgiven ourselves, released ourselves from past hurt and pain??? Answer! WE can't and this pain will always interfere with our emotions thus causing us to never truly love ourselves/others and in most cases blaming ourselves for things that have happened to us… Real love is not a feeling, real love is our actions and how we treat each other, how we are there for each other. What good is it to just lay with someone that really doesn't love you? Are laying with someone in vain just to be feel loved? Real love is not a feeling… Marriages today are so lost in the fact that the head over heels love you first had isn't the kind of love that is going to keep your marriage going into the happily ever after stage. A new level of love must evolve in your marriage, a love that is unbreakable, a love that is trusting, a love that is comforting, a love that is everlasting to everlasting, a love that is based on what I can do to help my spouse and not a love that is based on what can I get out of the marriage. Not a love that only buys roses in our wrong but a love that showers each other every day… Real love is action not feeling, a verb word that causes you to do, even after the I DO.

7.) **Aversion to discomfort (intimacy, hardship, struggle, physical and emotional pain, facing your own and your spouse's weaknesses, sacrifice).** We humans do not like pain/discomfort. We'll do almost anything to avoid or get out of pain. Relationships often bring pain and or discomfort with them as a matter of course. But know that with each pain, each struggle, the pressure that you are feeling right now as you read this book in wanting to walk out on it all, these things, if fought through the power of Jesus Christ can push your marriage into a high dimension. Marriages today are just given up because no one wants to fight anymore, with the first sign of pain, bags are backs and the fight is over with a door slamming in front of your soul-mate and that is not what God intended for marriage to be. We have to understand that anything worth having is worth fighting for. When you said I DO you promised to God and not man that you would be there in the good and the bad times and there is a blessing in fighting through the bad times. Anyone can enjoy the good times when there is no struggle, true love is demonstrated at the point of pain and discomfort and our we are able to handle those pains will determine how long we are married.

8.) __Not working to be friends (continuing the courtship).__ The hustle and bustle of life can cause us to make our marriage take a backseat, but it is at that point that we give up on our marriage unknowingly and in most cases forget about it. But, marriage is work and we must constantly spend time on it to mature it, shape it and mold it and we must put forth the effort and energy into that we did when we first starting dating our spouse, keep doing the special things we did to fall in love, find and do similar interest, do new things, take at least one trip a year without the children, somewhere fun and make the best out of it, become children yourselves again forgetting the pressures of the world and see how much in love you really are.

Chapter 9

Ephesians 4:31-32

Overcoming the Spirit of Bitterness in Marriage

Here are ten tips to overcome bitterness and resentment:

1. Ask God to forgive you for being bitter and resentful. Then ask him to forgive who   has hurt you. "For if you forgive men when they sin against you, your heavenly father will also forgive you. But if you do not forgive men their sins, your father will not forgive your sins. Matt. 6:14

2. Don't allow the bad that happened to keep you from God's best.

3. Don't enter a relationship or date because you will only hurt someone else.

4. Pray daily for God to heal you and research scriptures to study and apply to your life daily.

5. God will bring the justice. Your instruction is to forgive.

6. When you forgive you remove the offender's power to hurt you. Accept what has happened and understand you have to heal. Seek professional help if necessary

7. Understand that when we continue to walk around hurt and bitter, the people who have hurt us are hurting us every day and in most cases, have moved on and are enjoying life.

8. Allow God to help you forgive and forget. Some of us don't trust God; thus, we continue living in pain. Don't forget to continue to ask God to forgive who has hurt you. Ask God to bless their life and heal them as well.

9. Understand that forgetting means you are letting go of what they did to you. It does not mean you have amnesia.

10. Don't feel or act like you have to seek revenge. The Bible teaches us God will bring us our justice. He knows what was done to you and what you have done to others. "God will repay the exact compensation owed to us. He will settle and solve the cases of his people." Hebrews 10:30

Chapter 10

Exposing the Spirit of Jezebel in Your Marriage

The bible teaches us not to tolerate the spirit of Jezebel in Rev 2:18-29 because if we tolerate it, it is then held against by God himself. So we must expose this spirit early in marriage and in most cases long before we do get married because this spirit is the spirit of divorce/division...

We have been taught that this spirit can only operate through the woman, but that in-fact is false and this has given a diversion to this sprit to operate in the man more than woman causing more than 50% of marriages to fall to divorce because of this spirit.

This spirit operates on selfishness in a marriage causing the other part to suffer in emotions/love and loneliness and once these spirits at attached to the other mate then there will be little to no communication in the marriage, no touching in the marriage and no sex life in the marriage because this spirit has set in and both the wife and the husband is waiting for the other to make the first step in breaking the silence and lack of touch but by the time they realize what is going on, the division has set in and the cheating begins in most cases starting with the husband, but the wife is more subject to stepping out of the marriage based on emotion and just needing communication/attention leading to lusting the opposite sex, resulting in sex taking place.

Below is a chart to start exposing this spirit in your marriage so that it can be destroyed in the name of Jesus!!!

Marriage of Pearls

1. Jezebel must destroy those they are afraid of because they have a spirit of fear, others are a threat to their security or position, they are highly insecure but will not admit it, and anyone who may expose them is the enemy. So, you must be careful about telling your issues to someone else and also remove the fear in your marriage because she will use that fear to bring you into a state of insecurity in your marriage, having you going through emails, phones, voicemails, tracking of phones and every person you all come into contact with will seem as if your spouse is either sexually attracted to them, looking at them in a lustful way or the person is attracted to your spouse. Until you remove this spirit from your marriage, it will always be a question of "Who was he/she??" No marriage should operate this way and each time it does you are operating in a spirit of Jezebel and she is pouring poison into your marriage to destroy it… If you trust and love your spouse, this spirit should never exist in your marriage…

2. They are controlling, manipulative and subtle. They take credit for the accomplishments of others and have others overlooked. It will always seem like the marriage is one sided and credit is never given to both parties… There will always be someone being talked down to as if they're a child, no respect in the marriage. It's always go fetch, sit, jump, give me some money and the moment you see this spirit the manipulation will start with tears, striking an emotion inside of you that makes you feel sorry for the very person that has been destroying you and you end up staying and you only get along when you both are talking about someone else in a negative way… There is never any real love, real communication and the marriage will always be homeless, broken and financial ruined causing you to always lean on others for what you need…

3. Lying is necessary to protect themselves from mistakes they make (but blame others for). They lie, and they know they are lying. This is the ultimate weapon of Jezebel, this spirit will cause so much hurt, struggle and problems with just a lie and if there is constant lying in your marriage on either side for any reason, then your marriage is under the spirit of Jezebel and it must be dealt with and if the other party is un-willing to deal with it, then you must remove yourself from the marriage because it shall only destroy you and you will live a life of pain and regret because you've spent so many years un-happy and struggling…

4. They are narcissistic (in love with themselves only) and have no concern for the feelings of their victim. In fact they tend to play the role of victim themselves to gain support and sympathy. They are committed to only one thing – getting what they want no matter what the cost is to others. The victim in this case is the spouse and it seems no matter what the other spouse does, they can do no wrong, they can't see the wrong in themselves and anytime you speak of their wrong they get very defensive, yelling and arguing about something totally different than what you were talking about…
Also, let us understand that this spirit doesn't have to be in your spouse for it to destroy your marriage. This spirit can operate in those around you that you love and in a lot of cases it will operate in your in-laws causing division in your marriage…

Marriage of Pearls

5. They quietly record criticisms from others and then manufacture false accusations to be released in secret meetings behind their victim's back. Of course they do not see this as gossip but label it as "sharing a concern." This happens more with the wife than the husband, the wife will write down all her feelings on paper and when that isn't good enough she will vent out to close friends and family and depending on the person she is talking to, the conversation can very quickly escalate into gossip "another spirit" and marriage bashing because the person she tends to call is someone that hasn't been through anything, can't keep a man let alone get married and the man she is with, she treat like hell in public and she tends to act like she's never submitted to man in her life putting up this strong front and her envy for your marriage will soon be exposed through your un-happiness and secret meeting with her...

6. Absolutely masterful in attacking and denying, as jezebel will have you discredited or removed. Again, absolutely masterful in winning compassion and support from others by appearing to be an innocent bystander while making you look like the abusive attacker by manipulating you into frustration or anger. This spirit will often cycle between being the attacker and being a victim which is done purposefully to confuse you. Careful investigation must be made to distinguish the real victim from the fake (jezebel) one.

7. They rationalize and defend, but never admit they were wrong. The devil and his demons are masterful at masking, hiding and camouflaging. Therefore, in the husband and wife relationship, the jezebel spirit will launch its attack through the host during PMS (the Pre-Menstrual cycle). So yes, PMS affects the woman's hormone levels, associated body chemicals and therefore accomplishes mood swings (tension, irritability, crying spells, anxiety, depression), but… just as the military launches their attack at night, jezebel launches it's attack during PMS so no one suspects demonic activity by saying "it's just PMS" when the truth is that it is PMS and a whole lot more. Let us also, understand, that men also have PMS, they just don't bleed and this spirit will use him that that very time of the month as well.

8. They are usually women but can be men. The women tend to control their men with sex. They pick passive men so they can dominate them. Before the marriage, you and your spouse where having sex a lot and after the marriage it went from 20 times a month to 4 times a month, then once a month and now you are in a stage of begging to even have sex and when you don't beg and are not controlled then your spouse feels as if you don't love them or find them sexy anymore, but rather than put yourself through that emotional rollercoaster, you find yourself watching more porn and masturbating more to make up for the lack of sex with your spouse and the division is clearly there which means that Jezebel is present... The man should not always have to come to the wife for sex, there should be days where the wife plans something sexy for her husband and surprise him as he walks in the door from a hard day's work. The man likes to feel wanted as well, they have feelings and loved to be chased more than the woman does. But, in marriage when 1 person is doing all the chasing, it beings to drive all the fire out of that person and then the flame in your marriage has been put out because something God created to satisfy both parties has been placed as a controlled substance and given as deemed fit... Enjoy your love, sex life and take it out of the box you have placed it in because there will come a time when neither of you will be able even have sex and no one is promised tomorrow and you will be begging God just for one more touch from your spouse but it will have been too late and you will then realize how selfish you really were...

9. Jezebel will make false allegations and call the police. The father will get dragged through the courts multiple times in a few years. Each case involves hundreds of pages of documents that he has to answer as a result of new evidence or complaints and will spend days in court at a huge cost to defend himself. She will also use his children against him and use them as pawns to strike major blows into his heart and not let him see his children… He will try to change and the more he tried to be/do better, she will strike him down with words that can kill/destroy his dreams. This part of the spirit destroys your mind after the marriage has been destroyed. Yes, this spirit keeps destroying you even after it has destroyed your marriage. If, you allow it to do so!!!

10. Psychological counseling will not help because the individual will both deny what they are and deny they have the evil spirit of jezebel motivating and/or controlling them. Jezebel lacks the internal emotional mechanisms to have healthy relationships because they have been emotionally damaged in early childhood and are therefore emotionally and relationally underdeveloped. Think of the jezebel person as a "two-year-old." A child that has no idea of how to heal themselves after a painful, emotional incident and this is what is going on with most of the marriages today, people are getting married and never took the time to repair the damage that is within themselves, instead they get married, bringing extra luggage into the marriage with someone that already has a house full of luggage and there is know where to rest their bags and carrying them only makes you tired and once you get tired of carrying all that mess around with you, you begin to act out to take the focus off of you and cause more damage to your marriage and the marriage ends in divorce…

Marriage of Pearls

11. Under the control of a demonic spirit, the mental and emotional health of the jezebel will continue to deteriorate. The jezebel (sociopathic) mother will allow a new partner to sexually abuse a child in an effort to purposefully inflict emotional damage to the child and turn the child into a manipulative mini-me. The courts do not recognize the sociopathic woman as incapable of functioning as a mother nor does the court see the demonic aspect of the jezebel. The jezebel uses the child as a tool to manipulate and control the father and extract finances from the father. The father is left to helplessly watch as precious children suffer at the hands of their mother.

- **As I stated, this spirit can also reside in a man and I will breakdown this spirit in the man so that women can discern for themselves if they are indeed in a marriage with someone that has a spirit of Jezebel...**

The spirit of Jezebel in a man exposed...

- **Characteristics**

1. He targets them by falsely mirroring their values, interests, goals, philosophies, tastes and habits. He is "everything you are." Wow, you have so much in common! You are a too perfect match! He comes on strong, sweeping his victims off their feet. He can be a "hot, passionate lover." Women are flattered by his intense attention of them, and excited by his male dominant approach to sex. He sexually "adores" them in Romeo fashion.

2. He fakes integrity, honesty and sincerity. He convincingly mimics human emotions. He uses people. He is a "sincere liar."
3. He can seem very spiritual or idealistic, but this is superficial. His interpretation of scripture, however, may not agree with what God had in mind.

4. He can suddenly play the role of the victim. Similar to the sneaky charming jezebel. Victims take pity on him. They see him as needing them. He is playing on the natural nurturing character of women.

5. He can inspire the woman to attack those who are supposed to be victimizing him. This causes injury to innocent people, and hurts the woman's relationships with others. Her friends and family can be alienated from her in this way.

6. He wants to marry victims quickly. Impulsive. He wants his victims dependent on him. He portrays false integrity, appears helpful, comforting, generous.

7. The fake sincerity does not last as he starts to change into his true self. He will have numerous romantic relationships. He has no loyalty to anyone except his own body parts.

8. He blames others in the relationship. His victims are objectified and disposable.

This spirit, if, in a man can be very destructive, dangerous and in many cases life threatening and the sooner you can discern this spirit in the man, the sooner you are able to work on possibly saving your own life.

This spirit in a man with operate on a level of conflict and deception. This is the first level, kind of like a suicide bomber in the making... Internally, this man will feel damaged and out of control more often than not and will try to control and environment he is in just to feel some type of power or control...

This man will not trust others in any form and will always find and issue with someone to try and start and fight. In marriage he will fight with the wife over the smallest things because he really doesn't trust her and there is nothing she can do to make him trust her any more or any less. His spirit has already been set to trust no one because the spirit of Jezebel knows that if he beings to trust people there is a chance that the spirit controlling him can/will be exposed. He has major anger issues, insulting others is no problem for him to do and he can go from this nice peaceful man into a rage of fire in a matter of seconds...

Marriage of Pearls

This spirit loves to play people against each other and he loves to watch his work un-fold in-front of him. The destruction smells like roses as things are falling down but he always careful to keep his allies and target separate in fear of being exposed.

He will twist your words in any conversation, especially the bible, just so that he can initiate his view that he know Is wrong and will even try and strike fear into you just so that you will accept what he saying to be true…

He knows that religion is a useful tool and will use it to control others around them but he will never take it serious, to him it's just a means of controlling his wife and getting her to do as he wishes with no questions or push back from her…

This spirit in a man is so dangerous because in most cases the men that are operating in this spirit are angry or at war with God because of something that has happened to them in the past that they had no control over. For most men, it's the rejection of a mother or father; it can also be from them losing a loved one very close to them to a tragic accident causing death…

He not only makes threats but he will carry them out his self… He will find everything wrong with your friends so that you have no one you can turn to but him, giving him total control over you in more ways than one… This way he puts you in a place to need help and you'd have to seek him and he will in return deny you the help, further destroying you emotionally…

Prepare to get out of the way and put distance between you and them. Don't get involved in anything illegal. Trying to stop them may backlash with a cascade of retaliation. Or, prepare to defend yourself, because they will try to hurt you.

Environmental development scenarios:

Society – delinquent progresses to gangster, crime.

Family – rebellious child progresses to abusive adult, family problems

Church – unsaved person progresses to fake saved status, and causes problems in church, rebellion and sometimes church splits.

Workplace- misfit but borderline competent progresses to supervisory position by backstabbing.

Marriage – disagreeable, cheating spouse progresses to abusive spouse, divorce.

Politics – malcontent progresses to terrorist, dictator.

- **What to do about him:**

✓ Abandon your efforts to help or cure him.

✓ His true mask exposed and the false character he portrayed is gone forever.

✓ Accept the reality. He does not want to change. Any "I will change" is a lie.

✓ Seek therapy. Seek prayer and support. You are the only one that will want help. He is not concerned. He can get another woman using the same methods he got you.

✓ Ignore and don't react to his hurtful words. It is not your fault that you are not good enough for him. Do not let him blame you for the break up.

✓ Don't take the bait when he blames or lies. They fool even trained professionals. Check out what he says. Get proof.

✓ Do not be vulnerable or naive. Check out his past before you get involved with any man. Look at how he treats others.

✓ Prepare for a nasty divorce. He will slander you.

✓ Accept no abuse. Respect yourself. Learn to fight back.

✓ Do your homework before getting involved with someone. How does he treat other people? How does he treat his mother and sister? What does his father think of him? How does he get along with relatives? Co-workers?

✓ Do you hear many complaints from him about them? Do they complain about him? Does he lie? Does he take advantage of people? Does he respect others?

✓ Look at your own weaknesses that let him in. If you allowed the sex without the real love, then you need to work on that. Check your own value system and morals. He took advantage of your willingness to compromise your values. Work to correct your weaknesses. Close the door to his type.

Understand the biblical principle of bad tree = bad fruit, and good tree = good fruit. If you are not sure about the tree, look at the fruit. Before a woman gets deeply involved with any man, his behavior and moral character should be carefully examined.

Chapter 11

"Time to heal the Pastor's wife"

In this chapter we will go over the pain of a pastor's wife. Yes, the pain!!! The pain that she never talks about!!! The pain that makes her feel lonely!!! The pain that makes her go to sleep silently but crying!!! The pain that makes her question her marriage and question the love her husband has for her!!!

This destroys many marriages every day and separates the Pastor and his wife in the same home and most cases they live in separate homes and meet up on Sunday for service as one big happy family. Yes, there are a lot of Pastor's and 1st Ladies living separately because of all the strain the ministry has caused on their marriage... Below I will share with you a blog a 1st Lady posted, word for word with no alterations. You can feel the pain, strain, stress, depression through her words... It almost brought tears to my eyes as I read it in thoughts of thinking of my own wife and all that she does for not only our family but the ministry and how most people don't appreciate what she does and takes her for granted...

"I wish my husband would have included me in his life to be his cheerleader. I wish he would have respected my calling and ministry. I wish someone would have told me that he was going to neglect me and forget about our dreams as a married couple. Now he lives for the church. Birthdays and anniversaries do not exist in this home. I'm tired of eating dinners alone and having anniversary trips cancelled because he has no interest. What does he always tell me? Oh yeah, "The Kingdom of God is always first." Now even my faith in God is at question. How could God give me a husband who is a pastor and so easily live without me? I feel stuck in this marriage. I am unfulfilled as a woman, wife, minister, and mother. Everything he promised me he has broken. I wish someone would have told me it would be this way. Then maybe I would have paid more attention to my gut feeling!"

Wow!!! The pain is so obvious. The hurt is so deep!!!

Marriage of Pearls

1 Timothy 3:5: "If anyone does not know how to manage his own household, how will he take care of God's church?"

This text clearly tells us that the Pastor is supposed to take care of his home first and his should be at the top of the list... If they can't manage their own home they can't take care of the church...

Yes, Pastors are pulled in a million different directions and those directions are always far away from his wife but please pastors, don't neglect your soul-mate because to neglect them is to neglect yourself, to make them hurt is to make yourself hurt...

Satan's biggest goal is to destroy the man so that he can destroy marriages that God has put together and in destroying the marriage he also destroy the family and he'll use the spirits that the 1st lady is feeling to break down the marriage as he is breaking her down on the inside, but yet she still smiles in the face of the very people that are keeping her husband from her, the very people that call at all hours of the night for the smallest things, the very people that don't respect her and see her as just another woman in the church...

The title alone in most churches make her a different person before her husband is even called to pastor the church. Churches have today put the pastor's wife in a roll that makes her uncomfortable and more stressed.

The pastor's wife is supposed to always look nice, smile, sit down in the front row of church, and agree with her husband. Her kids need to be model Christians. She needs to be ready to open her home to people in the church at any time and serve them. It's good if she volunteers to play the piano, help in the children's ministry, or teach women's Bible study.

Yes, stereotype such as those are what cause her to hate the church, her husband and ultimately God.

The truth is that each pastor's wife is unique! But one thing that most pastors' wives have in common is that THEY HAVE A SIGNIFICANT AND CHALLENGING GOD-GIVEN OPPORTUNITY TO HAVE INFLUENCE FOR CHRIST IN A CHURCH AND THE SURROUNDING COMMUNITY. But to step into the role of pastor's wife, with all it's conflicting expectations and ministry stress, pastors' wives need a special grace and wisdom from God and they must be allowed to be themselves nothing else...

In most cases the pastor barely interacts with his wife at the church or even his children 99% of his time is devoted to the church and the people that hinders our marriage... The pastor is up late Saturday night studying and praying preparing for Sunday and his wife sleeps alone, he sleeps with her for a few hours and keeps up early Sunday morning goes to the church, puts on his robe, enters the pulpit with a huge smile on his face while his wife is hurting deep in her soul. Everyone is shouting as he preaches and she sits and gives an occasional wave at his hypocrisy. She laughs and smiles at his jokes feeling like a reserve cheerleader. She pretends to be happy when the fact is she is really depressed and desires to fall down at the Alter crying loud to God of her pain, but instead she sits in her front row seat silently asking God how long will she have to endure such pain and loneliness.

There is no more sexual intercourse in the marriage, no intimate kisses in the marriage and thoughts that her husband is cheating begin to roll through her mind, pushing her further away from him and God, the pain becomes excruciating with each tear that falls down her cheek and she feels un-sexy and attractive and begins to think that she is the problem that her marriage is failing, the reason why her husband won't touch her. She starts to drastically work to get back to the size she was before she had children but, he doesn't notice as she changes because he so submerged in the church she has become invisible to him.

Pastors' wives, just like every other church member, need discipleship, intentional care for their soul, and direction in ministry and they find women to study with.

Many women's Bible studies discuss how to become a "Proverbs 31 woman." AN EXCELLENT WIFE, WHO CAN FIND! These studies would also do well to caution women against becoming a "Proverbs21 woman." "It is better to live in a corner of the housetop than in a house shared with a quarrelsome wife. It is better to live in a desert land than with a quarrelsome and fretful woman" (Proverbs 21:9, 19). I like to joke with my husband that when I am "a quarrelsome and fretful woman" then he is in DOUBLE trouble. Our roof is less than habitable, AND we live in a desert!

Marriage of Pearls

Are you a quarrelsome and fretful wife? Are you the common denominator of dissension and strife in your home? Or are you a supportive and helpful wife? Are you building your home by God's grace in order to bring it under the headship of your husband to the glory of Jesus? Or do you foolishly tear down your home with your own hands (Proverbs 14:1)?

Many of the questions asked above can cause different spirits to enter your marriage and in most cases cause a communication breakdown in the marriage. Major ones such as, there is no communication when either spouse walks in the room and no hello kisses anyone or goodbye kisses anymore. Stubbornness/pride has set in the marriage and you both are waiting on the other to make the first move in communication, even in the communication of making love because you're allowing the spirit of divination to dictate your marriage based on how you feel and assuming your spouse feels a certain way instead of communicating your feelings to each other.

- **There will be spirits activating itself against your marriage through members of the church to try and separate you. These are the top spirits will operate through:**

1.) <u>Jealousy-</u> This spirits operates from a distance, talking about every part of your marriage, spreading lies about your marriage, spreading rumors, dropping destructive spirits in your marriage in hopes that they can destroy what God has put together so that they can slip in once the bond has a crack in it. They desire what you have and when someone desires what you have they will go to great lengths to destroy it and be there to pick up the pieces before they hit the ground... **#ProtectYourMarriage!!!**

2.) <u>Gossip-</u> In ministry people will always gossip about your marriage in hopes that it gets back to you and once it gets back to you, it then is up to you if the information has a place in your marriage or do you instantly destroy it through prayer. Nothing can manifest in your life without your approval and you entertaining it. Some things don't deserve to be addressed. The issue that those married and are in ministry make is they address the issue and want to put someone in their place. Once you do that, they know that they've got you out of your spirit/anointing and you are now playing their game and you've given them permission and the entry point to your marriage. Instead, keep silent, in all things, pray about it, fast and give it to God and watch him work things out for you…

3.) <u>Lust-</u> This spirit operates powerfully through most churches today and are geared toward the pastor/high ranking men of the church and to destroy this spirit, the pastor's spouse will have to be very strong/supportive/positive in herself/not jealous or easily swayed because this spirit will target the husband in provocative clothes in hopes to make the spouse think that the pastor took a look at her and then the fire has started and what she set out to do is now in motion. In ministry, the spouse is never to take a back seat in anything because that is what this spirit wants you to do so that they have free access to the pastor and in your marriage. Never allow anything to push you away from your husband/marriage. Yes, ministry takes a large toll on a marriage but remember your marriage was built for the ministry and nothing can tear it down but you, your spouse and God. Once either side gives into this spirit, they offer the marriage over to Satan to have his way with it. Instead rebuke this sprit and keep your marriage strong and give no room for lust in your marriage. Satisfy each other and take trips alone to places you've never been to and enjoy each other when time permits and in some cases you have to make the time because ministry is demanding but remember, your marriage always comes first.

4.) <u>Rejection-</u> The deepest need we all have is to be loved and cherished by someone that is very special/close to our hearts. However, the biggest pain/fear of a wife married to a man in ministry is rejection, not feeling loved, not hugged in her

Marriage of Pearls

time of need. Fear of being rejected when she has an issue she needs her husband for and not her pastor. Fear of not getting the attention she used to get from her husband before ministry. Fear of being ignored in the church and taken for granted and she feels as if everyone is stepping over her just to get to her husband as if she is a doormat to the house of God and door bell to the pastor office. Now she feels as if she is not even in second place with the church but that she has no place not only in the church but a place in her marriage.   These unhealthy feelings can make anyone response in an aggressive way that always spills out into open anger, displeasure and a simply I don't care attitude. But, she loves her husband so much that she doesn't want to do anything to hurt him or the ministry God has given him, so she internalizes everything inside of her and the fight gets so out of control that her organs are now fighting against each other and her body starts to breakdown from the inside causing more damage such as cancer, tiredness, abdominal pain, frequent headaches, loss of appetite and start to silently withdraw their love and affections towards her husband and church. Don't hold these feelings inside, instead tell your spouse how you are feelings but do it in a loving way that pleases God, a way that no one is raising their voices and we must learn to put our spouses above everything except God. Start to prioritize your marriage and the church functions so that there is more time spent with your spouse instead of at the church and counseling. Be more verbally affectionate towards each other. Be more physically affectionate to each other in public; let your love show to the world. That way no one person has to beg for kisses, hugs, or any kind of emotional intimacy in the marriage. Seek counseling if you need to but remember, it will only help if you both want to save your marriage.

5.) Envy- Continue to chapter 12 for the spirit of Envy.
Be careful not to allow these spirits in your marriage as they can and will destroy every part of your marriage if you tolerate them and don't address them. Be sure to always put your marriage above everything except God. Ministry life can be demanding, leaving no time for your spouse, but, you must make time for your spouse, even if that means you must put them on the schedule to ensure that it happens. Take trips out of the city away from the church and the strain of ministry. Pray without ceasing with each other and communicate your feelings to each other.

The healing process for the Pastor's wife must start because if she is not healed and her needs are not met, she will give up and she'll start saying the following like all other pastor's wives:

"I can't do this anymore."

"Ministry is not for me."

"I want to leave my pastor husband."

"My husband is a pastor but I don't want to be a pastor's wife."

"This is too hard."

"Help! My husband wants to be a pastor. What should I do?"

These are just a few of the desperate cries for help from the women married to men in the ministry. They smile, but, no one cares to even look behind the smile to see her real pain. They have this picture of what she is, what she is to wear and what she is to do. In most cases they dress her up in flashy clothes with big hats and make her out to be something that she is not. This adds more hurt to her already pin less grenade that is just waiting to explode, destroying any and everything in the area.

Marriage of Pearls

The urge to quit rises higher than ever when the enemy who likes to whisper destructive things in her ear begins to tell her:

"You're not making any difference."

"You'll never be able to minister to that person."

"All that criticism? That's who you are."

"You're a failure."

"Why do you even try? Those people don't even care about you."

"God isn't using you."

"God doesn't have anything special planned for you- just more of this non sensical mundane service that doesn't yield any results."

"You shouldn't be a pastor's wife if you struggle with that."

"You can't be a good mother because you're a pastor's wife."

"You don't have to take that abuse. Just look out for yourself, 'cause nobody else will."

Satan pushes the wife extra hard just to get in her head to get to the pastor. She will always face the hardest test. Just look at Adam and Eve and how Satan tempted her to get Adam to sin and ultimately being cursed for doing so.

Satan never seems to run out of insults and discouraging words. He seems to plant those words as seeds in her head or if he really wants to get to her he will use someone to do his dirty work. Because, face it!!! It hurts even more when it comes from someone else, especially someone that you are already dedicating your life to, someone that you are already losing your marriage to, someone that has already caused so much hurt and pain. Yes, Satan will use someone to get in your head and throw you off of everything God has for you to do and even making you feel like you have no place in the ministry with your spouse. When, in fact you are the key piece to the ministry.

We must understand that over 75% of Pastor's wives throw in the towel, the house, the car, the marriage and the church and walk away. Then there are some that keep the appearance of a pastor's wife looking good on the outside but, deep on the inside where deep meets deep in core of their heart and soul there are done and have quit. They can no longer deal with the pressure that is unfair to them, the countless women trying to destroy her marriage, the backstabbing by the congregants, the feeling of being walked on, stepped on, spit on, pushed, dragged, disrespected, left out, and feeling like a charity case. So, this strong, beautiful, graceful, intelligent, God fearing Queen retreats to the background without a word suppressing all of her pain quietly in a room full of light yet feels so dark and she gives up the battle to press on and Satan has won the battle and a greater battle has been lost.

Out of this dark and dry place God will use it and bring the greatest fruit out of your life to get the glory and render you double for your shame. Yes, he will use YOU!!! The person that feels unworthy, imperfect, hurt, destroyed, weak, tired, the exhausted you and meets you in the those places in your life, the place where you had given up and comes whispers in your ear and says: "Let's finish this together, just hold to my unchanging hand and I will lead the way my child."

1 Corinthians 15:58 (CEB)

[58] As a result of all this, my loved brothers and sisters, you must stand firm, unshakable, excelling in the work of the Lord as always, because you know that your labor isn't going to be for nothing in the Lord.

Chapter 12

Destroying Spiritual Insecurity

This spirit will cause you to think that negative things are happening in your marriage and in every area of your life. It destroys the integrity in your marriage by imparting lies, addictions, lust, envy, bitterness, anger, hopelessness and the list goes on.

There was a young couple that was married for only a year and found themselves having multiple trust issues. So much so that they were considering divorce and in the yelling's and door slams one cold morning at 3AM the door slams to the bathroom and with the wife now in the bathroom the husband is banging on the door while packing his suit case and he yells one final time, I am gone, have a nice life and as he grabs his suit cases she swings the door open, with tears in her eyes she screams "NO!!!" She falls to the floor in a panic and in a sobbing voice she says "I'm pregnant!!!" The husband drops his suitcases in disbelief and falls to comfort her but she pushes him away. Normally, this would be great news but this didn't make trust issues any better in their marriage. The husband stayed but the farther along she got the more insecure she became in the marriage.

She began to ask him questions about other women, if he thought they were pretty or not and in most cases the man never seen the woman until she pointed her out and before he could say no after she pointed the other woman out, she interrupts with a loud laugh "Yeah right!!!" She screamed!!! You don't even acknowledge me anymore!!! Then she storms off!!!

Many of our problems in our lives will no longer be a problem when we fully let God in our marriages. In most cases people want the marriage without God. Never accepted God but desires to wear a white dress down the aisle of a church. Never addressed the past hurt of your last relationship or never let go of the love and now you find yourself committing adultery before you even say I DO. God was never invited in your life to even connect to the soul of this marriage. Who's to say that the marriage you're in was put together by God??? You never asked him, you simply just said YES!!! Started crying and never expected that the tears would never end. Not understanding that with God all things work together for your good but without God nothing can function and will eventually be destroyed and possibly destroying your trust in others in the process.

Any insecurity, inferiority complex, or accusation never comes from God but from Satan. Those that are insecure for any reason will always overcompensate for their insecurities. Overcompensation may be the result of a person feeling that he/she has not been recognized I a way pleasing to them. Subconsciously he/she wants to cry/scream/yell out to their spouse, "Why don't you recognize me more? Is your porn sexier than me?!?! I am your wife/husband and I have real feelings, too. I want the same complements you enjoy. I need/demand to be noticed; please pay attention to me." But because he/she cannot come out and say those words, inside they start to feel destroyed and unwanted. Arrows of pain start fly from his/her mouth; those who are struck may define this as uncalled-for arrogance. The arrows are unnecessary; the accusations are just retaliations. Nevertheless, we live in a world of fear and everybody feels he has to protect himself. We naturally build up protective devices around ourselves and as soon as our shell is pierced, some emotions automatically shoot out. None of them are warranted, but it happens. Although some people seem arrogant, often their behavior discourages others from investigating what the arrogance represents. Usually it is just a cry out for love.

Marriage of Pearls

So, hold them more, spend more time with them and it a point to get away to a hotel once a month. Yes, you have a home but there is nothing like getting away from it all for a night and enjoying your spouse the way you did the moment you met them. Become those teenagers again, become what made you fall in love again, become the moments you saw sparkles in each other's eyes, become laughter that had you talking on the phones for hours until you feel asleep, become the friends that would walk and talk for miles and not realize that hours have passed, become that person with no worries and your relationship the most important thing in your life before your children.

When we get away from these things that brought us together, we begin to place some doubt and fear in the marriage/relationship and that is when insecurity steps in and tries to destroy what God has put together but that love you both first shared will be the love that brings your marriage through!!!

Keep this scripture close to your hearts and in your souls to bring your marriage stronger than ever. Place it up in your home in a frame letting everyone know that regardless of what we go through, we will STAND on this word and we will STAND on our LOVE!!!

1 John 4:18 – **There is no fear in love; but perfect love casteth out fear: because fear hath torment. He that feareth is not made perfect in love.**

Chapter 13

Building a Fierce Marriage

1 John 4:18-19- ESV "There is no fear in love, but perfect love casts out fear. For fear has to do with punishment, and whoever fears has not been perfected in love. We love because he first loved us."

Firstly, let us ask ourselves, is our marriage perfect? The answer should be no if you're truly open and honest in your marriage because there is no perfect marriage, you'll always have ups and downs in marriage because marriage is constant work and constant change with more giving than taking and that giving has to be 100% and not 50-50 because 50-50 will only have someone else picking up the slack of the other 50%.

Secondly, ask yourself, do I fear anything in this marriage? Do I fear my spouse is cheating because I feel insecure? Do I fear that I am no longer sexy to my spouse? Do I fear other people will find my spouse attractive? Do I fear our love for each other will fade away? Do I fear that the time I cheated will be our destruction? Does fear keep me from trusting my spouse? Does fear cause me to check their social media, text and emails? Does fear have me calling every hour? Does fear having me asking who's that in the background? Does fear cause me to not want my spouse going out with friends? Is fear the reason we argue? Does fear keep us from gagging our marriage with questions such as? "Are you happy?" "Do I satisfy you?" "How do you feel about us?"

I could go on and on and I am sure you can as well! But fear has a plan and that plan is to destroy any thought of success and anything especially anything God has created such as marriage...

Marriage of Pearls

Fear will strike an argument out of the smallest, dumbest things and before you know tongues are lashing because there is power of life and death in the tongue and this tongue is so powerful and it begins to shoot venom through the veins of the tongue and seeks to kill within a matter of seconds with words of hatred and anger and the only way it can be destroyed is through pure and perfect love.

Fear also seeks to arise and it's power comes to terrify and hurt cutting deep as the soul and it's penetrating your marriage through discordance and lack of understanding in the marriage and your marriage is out of the will of God and in most cases we get married in a church saying that we're honoring God and our marriage but we're really disrespecting both and cursing both the marriage and God and if our marriage is out of relation with God then fear has full authority to come in our lives, homes, spirit and marriage to try and destroy us...

There is nothing more dangerous and more likely to destroy your marriage than sitting in idle indulgence of fear and doing absolutely nothing to prevent this fear from fulfilling its hunger and its main course is destruction topped off with death for the ultimate enjoyment. Is your marriage on the plate of fear???
It's like a main on the 10th floor of a burning building and the fire department has created a way out for him and all he has to do is jump but he turns back to a fire destroying the whole building trying to see if there is another way out other than jumping because he is afraid of hikes, so jumping is not an option, so instead of the man overcoming his fear of hikes he turns and runs back into the burning building and the smoke overcomes him and he dies in his courage to defeat the fire. So, instead of addressing your fears in your marriage you try and find another way out because you fear that if you do then it could lead to the death of the marriage when in fact avoiding it and

allowing more fear to manifest in your marriage is sure way to kill your marriage.

God has not given us the spirit of fear, but of love and a sound mind. As our scripture says, there is no fear in love. Don't let fear enslave you or torment you through false love or impart distrust in your spirit and if these things have set-in, be of good cheer because perfect love will cast out such fear and give you peace that will destroy walls that you never knew where built from some things in your childhood that may have caused you pain. Fear is the total opposite of happiness and both of these emotions can never be in the same place at the same time without placing some hurt or depression in the atmosphere.

If your marriage is in a state of fear, begin to rebuild the walls of your marriage through God and invite him your lives and seek God more and he will begin to remove that fear and increase in love in portions and your marriage shall then be everlasting to everlasting until death do you part.

- **Barnes commentary says:** There is no fear in love - Love is not an affection which produces fear. In the love which we have for a parent, a child, a friend, there is no fear. If a man had perfect love to God, he would have no fear of anything - for what would he have to dread? He would have no fear of death, for he would have nothing to dread beyond the grave. It is guilt that makes people fear what is to come; but he whose sins are pardoned, and whose heart is filled with the love of God, has nothing to dread in this world or the world to come. The angels in heaven, who have always loved God and one another, have no fear, for they have nothing to dread in the future; the redeemed in heaven, rescued from all danger, and filled with the love of God, have nothing to dread; and as far as that same loves operates on earth, it

Marriage of Pearls

delivers the soul now from all apprehension of what is to come.

But perfect love casteth out fear - That is, love that is complete, or that is allowed to exert its proper influence on the soul. As far as it exists, its tendency is to deliver the mind from alarms. If it should exist in any soul in an absolutely perfect state, that soul would be entirely free from all dread in regard to the future.

Because fear hath torment - It is a painful and distressing emotion. Thus men suffer from the fear of poverty, of losses, of bereavement, of sickness, of death, and of future woe. From all these distressing apprehensions, that love of God which furnishes an evidence of true piety delivers us.

He that feareth, is not made perfect in love - He about whose mind there lingers the apprehension of future wrath, shows that love in his soul has not accomplished its full work. Perhaps it never will on any soul until we reach the heavenly world, though there are many minds so full of love to God, as to be prevailingly delivered from fear.

Remember that fear has no place in love and ultimatums' have no place in love because those invoke spirits of fear in our lives to stay or to go. Instead we should love with boldness and confidence in perfect love given to us through God. John 3:16- God so loved the world that he gave his only begotten son. God here shows us what giving is, what love is and what sacrifice is when we truly love someone. Love is giving up what you love the most to save someone other than yourself and in marriage we must give up things that we love that maybe causing strains/fear in our marriage so that we can save our marriage because there is no marriage until sacrifice is given in the marriage.

Jesus died so that we did not have fear of anything, even death.

Hebrews 2:14-15 Contemporary English Version (CEV)

[14] We are people of flesh and blood. That is why Jesus became one of us. He died to destroy the devil, which had power over death. [15] But he also died to rescue all of us who live each day in fear of dying.

Fear invokes a spirit of torment and in the Greek it translates to the word punishment and has fear always contemplating in the mind a form of punishment deserved for how one is feeling based on what was done to invoke the fear and in most cases it's someone stepping outside the marriage committing adultery and you stay together with the betrayal in the front of your mind thinking of ways to pay your spouse back and now you've stayed together in imperfect love because now you're thinking of punishment you can throw in their face to say we're even now and love doesn't work that way because if God was to hold our sins over our head we'd never see the kingdom of heaven but he has given us grace and we should allow grace to enter our marriage.

1 John 3:18-24
Little children, let us love, not in word or speech, but in truth and action. And by this we will know that we are from the truth and will reassure our hearts before him whenever our hearts condemn us; for God is greater than our hearts, and he knows everything. Beloved, if our hearts do not condemn us, we have boldness before God; and we receive from him whatever we ask, because we obey his commandments and do what pleases him. And this is his commandment that we should believe in the name of his Son Jesus Christ and love one another, just as he has commanded us. All who obey his commandments abide in him, and he abides in them. And by this we know that he abides in us, by the Spirit that he has given us.

Marriage of Pearls

1 John 4:7-12, 16b-19

Beloved, let us love one another, because love is from God; everyone who loves is born of God and knows God. Whoever does not love does not know God, for God is love. God's love was revealed among us in this way: God sent his only Son into the world so that we might live through him. In this is love, not that we loved God but that he loved us and sent his Son to be the atoning sacrifice for our sins. Beloved, since God loved us so much, we also ought to love one another. No one has ever seen God; if we love one another, God lives in us, and his love is perfected in us.

- *Why This New Testament Scripture Makes a Good Wedding Reading:*

THE AUTHOR OF 1ST JOHN SAYS THE WORD "LOVE" NO LESS THAN 38 TIMES IN HIS EPISTLE- THAT'S FAR MORE THAN ANY OTHER BOOK OF THE BIBLE! SO, THERE ARE SO MANY BEAUTIFUL PASSAGES IN THIS BOOK THAT MIGHT BE APPROPRIATE FOR A MARRIAGE CEREMONY. MANY PEOPLE CHOOSE JUST 1 JOHN 4:7-12 AS THEIR READING, LEAVING OUT THE LAST FEW VERSES WHICH ARE PROBABLY THE MOST IMPORTANT VERSES. BUT ENDING THEIR OMITS A POWERFUL SENTENCE: "THERE IS NO FEAR IN LOVE, BUT PERFECT LOVE CASTS OUT FEAR." THINK ABOUT THAT SENTENCE AND ABOUT TIMES IN YOUR LIFE WHEN FEAR HAS GOTTEN IN THE WAY OF LOVE. IT MIGHT HAVE BEEN WHEN YOU WERE AFRAID OF BEING WRONG, AND COULDN'T ADMIT TO YOUR MISTAKES. IT MIGHT HAVE BEEN WHEN YOU WERE AFRAID OF COMMITMENT, OR EVEN WHEN YOU WERE AFRAID OF BEING VULNERABLE. MARRIAGE ALONE DOESN'T CONQUER THIS PROBLEM. WE'VE ALL HEARD

OF MARRIED COUPLES *fighting over money*, *jealousy* AND MOST OF THIS IS CAUSED BY THE SPIRIT OF INSECURITY. AT THE ROOT OF THESE FIGHTS IS A SPIRIT CALLED FEAR. WHEN WE CAN REALIZE THAT THERE IS NO FEAR IN LOVE, WE CAN WALK TOGETHER THROUGH ANY PROBLEMS, ANY ISSUES AND WE WILL OVERCOME WHATEVER COMES AT US, BUT THE WORLD HAS CREATED A GENERATION THAT DESIRES TO RUN AT THE VERY SIGHT OF A PROBLEM AND THIS SHOWS THAT THERE WAS NEVER LOVE THERE TO START WITH. THIS IS THE VERY REASON YOU HAVE PEOPLE SECOND GUESSING GETTING MARRIED ALL THE WAY UP TO THE MOMENT OF SAYING I DO AND THEY FEEL LIKE AT THIS POINT IT'S TOO LATE TO BACK OUT AND YOU'VE SPENT TOO MUCH MONEY ON THE WEDDING AND YOU DON'T WANT TO LET YOUR FAMILY DOWN OR MAKE THEM MAD BECAUSE YOU DON'T WANT TO GET MARRIED SO OUT OF FEAR YOU STAND AT THE ALTAR SHARING IN VOWS THAT YOU REALLY DON'T MEAN OR KNOW/UNDERSTAND WHAT THEY MEAN AND YOUR MARRIAGE IS IN A FIGHT BEFORE YOU EVEN SAY I DO BECAUSE IN YOUR MIND YOU DON'T AND THERE WAS NO MARRIAGE COUNSELING TO ADDRESS THE PROBLEMS IN THE MARRIAGE SO THEY WERE JUST SWEPT UNDER THE TABLE SO BY THE TIME YOU GET TO A YEAR IN YOUR MARRIAGE THERE HAS BEEN SO MUCH MORE SWEPT UNDER THE TABLE AND THE TABLE HAS BECOME ROCKY AND AT THE POINT OF FALLING OVER AND IF ONE MORE THING IS PLACED UNDER THAT TABLE IT WILL FALL OVER AND IN SOME CASES BREAK TO NO REPAIR CAN BE MADE TO IT. ADDRESS THE ISSUES THAT ARE CAUSING YOU FEAR UPFRONT AND DON'T WAIT UNTIL IT'S TOO LATE.

- **Revelation 19:1, 5-9**

Marriage of Pearls

After this I heard what seemed to be the loud voice of a great multitude in heaven, saying, "Hallelujah! Salvation and glory and power to our God,
And from the throne came a voice saying, "Praise our God, all you his servants, and all who fear him, small and great." Then I heard what seemed to be the voice of a great multitude, like the sound of many waters and like the sound of mighty thunder peals, crying out, "Hallelujah! For the Lord our God the Almighty reigns. Let us rejoice and exult and give him the glory, for the marriage of the Lamb has come, and his bride has made herself ready; to her it has been granted to be clothed with fine linen, bright and pure"— for the fine linen is the righteous deeds of the saints. And the angel said to me, "Write this: Blessed are those who are invited to the marriage supper of the Lamb." And he said to me, "These are true words of God."

- **TO REMOVE THIS FEAR IN YOUR MARRIAGE YOU MUST:**

1.) WORSHIP TOGETHER- GOD IS READY TO DO A SUPERNATURAL THING IN YOUR MARRIAGE BUT UNDERSTAND THAT GOD IS THE SUPER AND YOUR MARRIAGE IS THE NATURAL AND HE CAN'T DO ANYTHING WITHOUT YOU BOTH COMING TO HIM IN WORSHIP TOGETHER AS ONE AND THEN YOU'LL PLACE A HIGH PRIORITY ON NOT ONLY SPENDING TIME TOGETHER BUT SPENDING TIME IN THE PRESENCE OF GOD THROUGH WORSHIP. GOD DESIRES FOR YOU TO DO THIS IN A COOPERATE SETTING WITH OTHER WORSHIPPERS AND EVEN IN THE PRIVACY OF YOUR OWN HOME. WORSHIP GOD!!!

2.) PRAY TOGETHER- PRAYER IS A PLACE OF DEEP INTIMACY AND WILL DRAW YOU TO CLOSER TO EACH OTHER AS WELL AS GOD. IT WILL CALL THE DEEP THINGS OF YOUR MARRIAGE INTO THE WILL OF GOD. IT WILL START TO BUILD YOUR MARRIAGE UP STRONGER THAN IT EVER WAS THROUGH THE POWER OF GOD… THE DEEPER YOU BOTH GO INTO PRAYER THE DEEPER YOU GROW WITH GOD IN SPIRIT AND THESE PRAYERS WILL BREAK ANY CURSES SPOKEN OVER YOUR MARRIAGE THAT MAYBE CAUSING THE CONFUSION OR FEAR… PRAY TOGETHER!!!!

3.) STUDY TOGETHER- STUDYING THE WORD OF GOD TOGETHER WILL BRING YOU BOTH INTO AN UNDERSTANDING OF GOD'S WORD AND GROW AS ONE TOGETHER. HAVE DIALOGS OF THE SCRIPTURES THAT HAVE BEEN "PRAY" READ AND CEMENT THESE SCRIPTURES IN YOUR HEARTS, MIND AND SOUL. STUDY TOGETHER!!!

Chapter 14

DESTROYING STRONGHOLDS

II CORINTHIANS 10:4-5- [4] (for the weapons of our warfare are not of the flesh, but mighty before God to the casting down of strongholds),

[5] casting down imaginations and every high thing that is exalted against the knowledge of God, and bringing every thought into captivity to the obedience of Christ;

We must identify all strongholds in our marriage if our marriage is to ever be healthy but we must first know what a stronghold is.

- **What is a stronghold?**

A stronghold is a faulty thinking pattern based on lies and deception.

Deception is the number one tool for the enemy to use against you because it causes you to put your imagination to work and you begin to build this story of how you think things are and the devil uses your imaginations to start building blocks for a stronghold to be placed on your marriage. These types of strongholds will block our spiritual vision and cause us to destroy what God has blessed us with. Then the enemy will begin to invoke feelings in a place where your feelings are supposed to be safe and protected because you're in a marriage/partnership/covenant with each other and you don't expect to be lied on, gossiped about, ridiculed, deceived, or attacked with venomous words of hatred, instead you want to the total opposite of this and so does your spouse.

If we lived in a perfect world we wouldn't have spouses tearing each other down but since we don't the heartbreaking truth is this is happening in millions of homes across the world and in some cases words turn to violence and no one stops to realize there is a strongholds causing my spouse to put me in a choke hold.

Dr Fred Lowery, author of the book, **Covenant Marriage: Staying Together for Life**, wrote the following on this issue:

"You've got to build a safety net —an atmosphere so that each person is able to be honest. I can say what I feel. I can express my feelings, my emotions, knowing that I'm not going to be made fun of, laughed at, or put down or taken advantage of. You build that kind of closeness.
"It's pulling back the layers of our life because you're safe with that person —that one person where you can open the shutters of your life and be absolutely real, knowing that you're going to be loved in that process. There is no greater key to marriage than safe communication, because if you can't communicate, you can't have a great marriage."

My goal in this chapter is to expose all strongholds so that your marriage can flow freely with the love of God. To inspire everyone reading this book to tear down every stronghold on your marriage, break every chain of lust, and destroy every imagination spirit so that your marriage is soul connected and in the spirit and love God created it.

A stronghold is a fortress, a place that has a strong defence system in place and in most cases we build our strongholds in previous relationships/marriages and forget we ever built them and it shows up in our attitude when our new spouse does something that's reminds us of our old relationship. If you've placed up walls because you've been hurt in the past, destroyed in the past, touched in your childhood, raped, molested, taken for granted or whatever the case may be, **YOU NEED TO DESTROY THOSE WALLS RIGHT NOW!!!!!**

Keeping those walls up will never let/allow you to love or be loved how you deserve to be loved and you will taint everything that God puts in front of you that was intended to bless/increase you. No man/woman will ever be perfect enough for you, you will always find fault in them the moment you sense that you love them and you will activate the walls of protection and begin to slowly cause arguments over the smallest things to protect yourself but hurting the other person in the process.

A stronghold is "okuroma" in the original Greek (taken from 2 Cor. 10:3-5 and other scriptures), defined as the arguments and reasoning that you will use to defend your position or belief regarding something. This easily translates into the logic and reasoning, rationalization, and justification you will use to defend your right to make a choice that disobeys God and then try to make excuses for why you did it. The former sentence is exactly how I define strongholds in all three books. I give a very clear "example" of how a stronghold is formed using the command of Ephesians 4:26, do not let the sun go down on your anger. Christians disobey that command every day and then try to rationalize and justify why they have done so. Ephesians 4:27 (AMP) says that when you do that, you have just given the devil room, opportunity, and a foothold in your life. The enemy attacks and hammers through these open doors or opportunities in your soul, created when you try to rationalize and justify disobeying God (rather than repenting and turning away from the sin). I hope this clears up any misunderstanding. - Rev. Liberty Savard

We make everything the devil's fault and in most cases the fault is our own and we're terrified to look in the mirror of self and address the person we see and the longer we don't address the person in the mirror the more the our spirit attaches to the strongholds in our lives and becomes more powerful because we're feeding this spirit through our selfish pride.

Strongholds are the number one destroyer of every marriage because it seeks out the weakest area of your marriage/life to grab hold to, that area that is never talked about, that area that is never noticed until it's too late, that are that we pretend that's not there, that area of Lust, that area of Pride, that area, of Envy, that area of Selfishness, that area of Fornication, that area of Anger, that area of Short temperedness and we must all comes to agreement that we all have strongholds in our lives. Most of them stem from childhood abuse and if you find yourself married to someone that has been abused in their childhood, you must be patient with them as they're fighting not only to **BE SET** free but they're fighting to truly love and feel true love from YOU, their spouse. You must be compassionate with their situation, be loving but let your love only be aggressive in helping them destroy these strongholds from their childhood because once you help them destroy these strongholds you then set them free and save your marriage.

If you are a victim of childhood abuse, you have been dealt a MIGHTY blow by the enemy and you've been walking around with this spirit in you for years and feel there is no need to address it or even acknowledge that it's even there, so you try to place it in a lock box of "This never happened" but it DID!!! You will live in bondage for the rest of your life, leaving waves of destruction and destroying relationships along the way unless you do what God requires you to do. You MUST surrender your entire past to God and stop resisting to be delivered from your pain. You must change your way of thinking that everything being said is an attack or abuse towards you. You must stop preparing/setting your mind/spirit to be abused and looking for it in every conversation. You must stop wearing abuse like a Gold medal around your neck. You must stop living as a victim and start living as a victor. It is your time to be healed!!!

If not handled properly, you will find yourself in divorce court and divorce is stronghold the enemy loves because that means his mission has been accomplished. YES, Divorce is a stronghold. It is rebellion against God to not forgive someone, to be bitter against someone, to think you are better than someone, and to refuse to obey God because you think you are right. It is rebellion to divorce your spouse.

"For this reason a man will leave his father and mother and be united to his wife, and the two will become one flesh. So they are no longer two, but one. Therefore what God has joined together, let man not separate." When they were in the house again, the disciples asked Jesus about this. He answered, "Anyone who divorces his wife and marries another woman commits adultery against her. And if she divorces her husband and marries another man, she commits adultery." Mark 10:7-12 (NIV)

Then you ask, why then are the children of God divorcing at a higher rate than ever before. That's another chapter in itself but to explain a little bit, it's really simple, you have so many false prophets teaching God's children and God's children have not taken time to study the word themselves to realize they have rebelled against God and have erected walls/strongholds and have given Satan the keys and authority to control their lives.

Most will operate in strongholds of a "Closed Spirit" this is a spirit of bitterness and this spirit will block them from receiving anything positive, see/hear the truth. Everything will always be a lie, everything will always be prejudged. This closed spirit will literally build walls in-front of their spouse causing themselves to be shut off from the spouse and God and will separate themselves into another room cutting off any communication with the spouse and sometimes the children in the home feel this spirit at work and it will begin to make the children feel differently.

Anything the spouse does will be listed as bad in the mind of a person under this spirit. No amount of truth or kindness will destroy the walls of a person with a closed spirit… It takes an act of God to penetrate a closed spirit. Apostle Paul was a great example of one working in a closed spirit and had no intentions on doing anything the biblical way or hearing the truth. Instantly he was transformed on the road to Damascus from a spirit closed to all Christians. When Christ is your Lord, NEVER write off anyone. God can change anyone's heart.

Sometimes we must pull over to remove things that came from someone else.

- **Here are some strongholds that are destroying marriages today:**

Abandonment- This spirit brings about rejection or being forsaken, feeling as a cast away, unloved, deep hurt and unwanted. **Isaiah 54:6-** The LORD will call you back as if you were a wife deserted and distressed in spirit-- a wife who married young, only to be rejected," says your God.

Absalom- This spirit operates strongly in pride, seduction, rebellion betrayal, self-promotion ending in self destruction destroying everything around it. See II Samuel 15

Abuse- This is a spirit of mistreatment, perversion causing sexual abuse, rape, incest, molestation and mental abuse causing mind control. This spirit also operates in religious abuse or bible bullying, using the word to get the selfish results that they're seeking. If you feel walked over, then you're a victim of this spirit.

Accusation- This spirit operates in slander, jealousy, finger-pointing envy, hatred, judging and false accusations.

Addictions- This is a very destructive spirit and can cause physical abuse if not dealt with. This spirit operates in obsession, alcohol, drugs, "legal/illegal", Idolatry, selfishness and this spirit rest in whatever you crave and it does so right in your stomach through your mouth, nose, taste buds and throat and the main stream they use is rejection.

Adultery- Lust, fortification, unfaithfulness, whoredom, lying, deception and backsliding are the area this spirit operates in. This spirit works solely through the eyes to cause lust to set in and works closely with the spirit of Jezebel with the intention to shame or destroy a marriage through an extramarital affair.

Anger- This spirit operates in fury, rage, hatred, indignation, wrath, bitterness, un-forgiveness, retaliation, spite, revenge and outrage.

Marriage of Pearls

Beware when your marriage has this spirit active at work because, this spirit will cause deadly fights and can hurt more than just those involved, it can hurt the children and other loved ones that are trying to defend/protect you from this spirit.

Brokenhearted- This spirit operates in past or present hurt that causes sorrow, sadness, crying, bruised, wounded, disappointment and depression.

Camouflage- This is a spirit where everything is hidden to make it seem as everything is going great in the marriage to other people and will look great on the outside but it totally different in the homes of couples that have this spirit working in their marriage. It operates to conceal, disguise, deceive, wears a mask and between the marriage couple the true love everyone else is commending them on is really hard to find to them.

Cursing- This spirit strikes the smallest arguments into some of the biggest by using profanity, mockery, bitterness, anger and pride.

Failure- This spirit comes from curses in your bloodline where other married couples didn't make it and ended up in divorce or they stayed together was clearly unhappy with each other. It operates in defeat, frustration, suicide, depression, confusion, rejection and sadness. This spirit will keep you from loving hard in fear of being hurt. II Timothy 1:7- For God hath not given us the spirit of fear; but of power, and of love, and of a sound mind.

False- This spirit invokes false love, false personality, and deception, made to believe that something is real when it really isn't real and it is best to catch this spirit before the marriage because this spirit will take years you can't get back and cause pain that will hard for you to get healed from.

Fear- Fear of making decisions that is wrong for your marriage. Rejection, fear of responsibility in the marriage, this spirit can/will cause pain, sickness, cancer, confrontations and in some cases, people are in fear of having children because they fear they will not be a good parent to the child and some fear they will fail as a wife or husband just like their parents did, but you must be the one to rebuke fear and release your bloodline from the curse of fear in a marriage and create a marriage of love from God.

In-laws- Yes, these are people but it is very important that your in-laws are in agreement with your marriage or they will be the ones that see to it that destruction is placed in your marriage and they will operate in several spirits ranging from deceit, lies, intimidation, rudeness, bitterness, envy, strife, malice, with the biggest and strongest one being **"MANIPULATION"** with a driving force of gossip trying to destroy your marriage through the power of speaking ill of your spouse on late night phone calls and they will certainly work in the spirit of camouflage when they're around you to make it seem as if they like you and will even use the word love to bring you into an emotion that they do care and if they know you've been rejected by your family they will use that to pull you in closer and they're only pulling you closer because they want to see your broken heart when it falls through your chest. This can also invoke manipulation to be placed on your children as well and in some cases, the in-law will try and talk your children against your marriage and this will cause the spirit of rebellion to rise up in your children.

Insecurity- This spirit uses those with low self-esteem, causing them to be in fear of what others think, or causing them to feel not worthy of the person they're married to because they feel un-beautiful never seeing the true beauty within themselves, causing an extreme amount of self doubt, shyness and uncertainty in one's self, life and love.

Marriage of Pearls

Deal with this spirit immediately!!! Your marriage is falling because you are allowing this spirit to live in you and in it!!!

Jealousy- This spirit is very destructive and will cause some people to walk away because it's destructive and nerve racking. This spirit operates in envy, suspicion that will have you always going through your spouse's phone, emails, social media pages and even looking over their should to see what they are looking at on the laptop, it will have you questioning who they're talking to on the phone and even have you looking at the history on the computer to see what internet pages they have visited. It also operates in resentment, bitterness, paranoia, distrust, Insecurity, selfishness and hatred. Remove this spirit immediately as you can see it can be quite time consuming and tiring for the person that has this spirit, so imagine if you will how your spouse is feeling by having to deal with this spirit in you.

Jezebel- See previous chapters on this spirit.

Lack- This spirit operates in the form of poverty, not enough, financial problems and invokes the spirit of mammon on your money. Break this curse NOW!!!

Lust- This is a very powerful one as it invokes many spirits into your marriage such as desire for others, burning passion causing sexual dreams for someone else, impurity, masturbation, perversion, fantasy, wandering eyes, lust of the
eyes, abuse, adultery, craving, greed and so many more. Remember, you need to do what you did to get your spouse in order to keep your spouse. There is no letting your body go, stay in the gym, keep yourself together, make time for each other and the more appealing you stay, the less chance lust has of getting your marriage.

Pornography- This exotic, A-rated spirit destroys marriage everyday and it is not just men that fall victim to this spirit. A lot of women who were molested in their childhood have an addiction to porn more so than most men do rather it this spirit draws you in with lust, perversion, peep shows, anal sex, oral sex, orgies, bisexual, prostitution understand this is a marriage destroying spirit and it will not stop until it has fulfilled its selfish desires and making your marriage unclean. This spirit makes your spouse feel unwanted, un-needed, un-sexy and if you've fell deep enough into this spirit, you'll find yourself, pleasuring yourself more than you pleasure your life, you will spend more time watching porn than anything else in the world, even if you have to watch at work taking a chance of getting fired but this spirit doesn't care about your job because it doesn't have bills or mouths to feed… Break this spirit RIGHT NOW or it will destroy you and everything/everyone you care about including your children!!!!

Selfishness- This spirit is all about self, just as the name says. It is all about self love, stinginess, rejection and regardless of the situation everything will end up being about them. If you desire to better your life they will find away to make it about them being rejected and make you question if you really need to be better or not. This spirit wants things their way or no way, it wants you to want things their way and if things are not going their way, they will then get the spirit of a child and throw the biggest tantrum you have ever seen, slamming doors, cursing, sleeping on couches and they will wake up the next morning as if everything fine and nothing happened.

Stress- Stress in a marriage can cause cancer to rise up in the marriage and place a heavy burden on it that no couple can carry and will get heavier and heavier until the marriage is destroyed, someone dies or they seek God to lift this spirit from them. It operates through tension, worry, mental break downs, anxiety, strokes, cancer in the stomach and nervous breakdowns and all of these are very dangerous to the body and your marriage. The sooner you destroy this spirit the better off your marriage will be. This spirit also brings in outsiders into your marriage that don't want to see your marriage prosper or make it and they will use whatever you tell them to convince you to leave your marriage. BE careful of what you tell people... Not everyone is for you or your marriage and in most cases, they're envious and bitter at your marriage because they have not found love and that is only because they've fallen into the grips of bitterness and hatred and can't even love themselves.

Temper- **The bible tells us to be slow to anger... Proverbs 14:29** Whoever is patient has great understanding, but one who is quick-tempered displays folly.
This spirit is everything but patient and seeks to rise up at the smallest things in your marriage. Most people with this spirit are irritated very quickly and snap at you making you feel less than they really are. It's a form of intimidation such as that of dog who has been beaten and each time the master comes in the room the dog tucks his tail and runs to the nearest corner and lives miserable and in fear while they're there and seeks every chance to run away and just like that dog, you're tucking your tail, running to the nearest corner but you never seek away out because you're in fear for your life and your spouse has made you feel as if there is nothing else out there for you and that you are worthless. But that is not true, God has made you great and desires that you are treated as the King or Queen he made you to be...

Remember, these are just a few of the strongholds that can be on your marriage and some of the major ones that invoke other spirits of destruction. If you feel there are more in your marriage, make a list of those spirits and start to pray them out of your marriage. If they feel too strong for you to defeat, seek help from your pastor for prayer and counseling if it is needed...

"The Spirit clearly says that in later times some will abandon the faith and follow <u>deceiving spirits</u> and things taught by demons" (1Timothy 4:1, emphasis added).

"To appoint unto them that mourn in Zion...the garment of praise for the <u>spirit of heaviness</u>" (Isaiah 61:3, KJV, emphasis added).

"For ye have not received the <u>spirit of bondage</u> again <u>to fear</u>, but ye have received the Spirit of adoption, whereby we cry, 'Abba, Father'" (Romans 8:15, KJV, emphasis added).

"As for you, you were dead in your transgressions and sins, in which you used to live when you followed the ways of this world and of the ruler of the kingdom of the air, the <u>spirit who is now at work in those who are disobedient</u>"(Ephesians 2:1,2, emphasis added).

"And the <u>spirit of jealousy</u> come upon him, and he be jealous of his wife, and she be defiled" (Numbers 5:14, KJV, emphasis added).

"Dear children, this is the last hour; and as you have heard that the antichrist is coming, even now many antichrists have come...They went out from us, but they did not really belong to us. For if they had belonged to us, they would have remained with us; but their going showed that none of them belonged to us... But <u>every spirit that does not acknowledge Jesus</u> is not from God. This is the <u>spirit of the antichrist</u>" (1 John 2:18, 19; 4:3, emphasis added).

"As it is written: 'God gave them a <u>spirit of stupor</u>, eyes so that they could not see and ears so that they could not hear, to this very day" (Romans 11:8, emphasis added).

"And when he had called unto him his twelve disciples, he gave them power against <u>unclean [foul, lewd] spirits</u>" (Matthew 10:1, KJV, emphasis added).

Marriage of Pearls

"The Lord has mingled within her a <u>spirit of confusion</u>; and they have made Egypt stagger in all her doings as a drunken man staggers in his vomit" (Isaiah 19:14, RSV, emphasis added).

According to 2 Corinthians 10:5, strongholds must be destroyed. They are not to be remodeled. They are not to be repainted or covered with wallpaper. They are to be destroyed. Stop trying to fix up your strongholds to look pretty and just deal with them before they deal with you!!! Begin to purify yourselves in the blood of Jesus, repent for your sins and seek God in prayer…

James 4:8 says "Cleanse your hands, you sinners; and purify your hearts, you double-minded." Cleansing our hands refers to the outward manifestation of the stronghold, while purifying our hearts refers to the inward dimension.

Prayer against strongholds!!!

Dear God,

I lift up Men/women with broken hearts on today God. Husbands/Wives who feel mistreated or taken advantage of! Abandoned!!! Left for dead!!! I pray that you restore their hearts and their minds right now in the mighty name of Jesus. Grab husband's/wives hearts and transform them! Break any strongholds that the enemy has including addiction, alcoholism, workaholics and negative attitudes right now in the name of Jesus!!! Break the chains of poor health, foolishness, and poverty. Loose the grip of cancer, disease, slavery, and bitterness. Lord reconciles husbands/wives to their spouse. Redeem the promise they made at the altar and the love that motivated that promise in Jesus' name AMEN!

Chapter 15

Overcoming the spirit of Potiphar's wife.

Genesis 39:1-20

This spirit has an appetite for things that clearly does not belong to them and will cause imprisonment and destruction when they don't get what they desire. The spirit that desires sex with someone other than their mate and will lie on you when you tell them no. We must expose this spirit because, it is a powerful one destroying marriages across the world because spouses are never told of the sexual advances by others and when the lies start, it becomes too late to explain why you never told your spouse about the harassment.

Just like Eve gazing at the forbidden fruit, here is Mrs. P undressing this handsome, muscular and well-built Hebrew slave. She didn't beat around the bush, she flat out said: "Come to bed with me!" I am sure she was so brazen and beautiful that she felt that she could proposition men whenever and where ever she pleased and very few men turned her down, which explains her outraged when Joseph turned her down and the spirit of rejection kicked in. Joseph told her, "How then could I do such a wicked thing and sin against God?" (Genesis 39:9). Joseph didn't call her wicked; he called adultery wicked. And he made it clear who would be dishonored if he said yes. However, her desire to have him didn't stop her from trying even stronger. So much so Joseph refused to even go around her.

There are people out there that desire your spouse as desperate as an Egyptian housewife, someone with blind ambitions, unquenchable desire to have your spouse, endless lustful dreams about your spouse, it becomes a driving need that refuses to be ignored and unfulfilled waiting for the house to be empty so that she could make her move.

She grabbed him by his cloak and said "Come to bed with me!" Joseph ran from the house as fast as he could leaving his cloak in her hand. But she would not be denied, she caught him… Genesis 39:12 says she grabbed or took, in Hebrew it would mean like someone gripping sword and using it as a weapon.

She told Joseph twice to come to bed with me, translated terms such as: "Make love to me!" "Have sex with me!" People simply just want what you have and you must do all you can to protect your marriage from people like this. Just like Joseph, deny and even run if you have to but make sure your marriage is protected and clothed even when a piece of clothing has been taken, clothed your marriage in Isaiah 61:10: I delight greatly in the LORD; my soul rejoices in my God. For he has clothed me with garments of salvation and arrayed me in a robe of his righteousness. as a bridegroom adorns his head like a priest, and as a bride adorns herself with her jewels.

Covering your marriage in God righteousness will always cover those trying to destroy your marriage in a mantel of shame!!! That still didn't stop her from feeling rejected and having the spirit of blackmail, telling first her servants and then her husband who the bible says burned with anger. People with this spirit are most effective when they have too much time on their hands, or they envy your marriage and are not getting enough attention from their spouse and the flesh takes over in restlessness, envy, jealousy, bitterness and just a desire to fulfill and destroy all at once.

- **Let's expose the characteristics of this spirit:**

1.) Proud look.

2.) **Lying tongue.**

3.) **Seductive.**

4.) **A desire to kill innocent people.**

5.) **Feet that rush off to do evil.**

6.) **Causes swath discord among brethren.**

I urge you to stay away from this spirit! Don't associate with her in any form because she will only set you up for destruction in hopes of getting what she desires from you bringing pain and so many problems into your marriage.

Pay attention and listen to the wisdom God desires for you to have when dealing with this spirit. The lips of a married woman maybe as sweet as syrup and smooth as cool whip, with her kisses as soft as feathers, but when she is done, she is promised to leave you with a very bitter taste I your mouth and a sharp pain in your heart. She walks a road of death and desires to take your soul with her on her journey of destruction. STAY AWAY FROM HER!!! Stop opening the door for her!!! She comes through the front door and not the back; she is very bold walking past your spouse just to get to you.

The only god that this woman knew was her physical body and its lustful hunger! Despite the fact that she did not know this God of Joseph, she still broke a cardinal rule of the society in which she lived - the rule was this: women could belong to only one man - she could not in any way, shape, or form be involved in infidelity - although men had no such restriction - they could have numerous wives and even concubines!

Potiphar, himself, was engaged in a sin of omission! The argument could be made that Potiphar should have been more attentive to his spouse! He should have recognized her needs and pursued a course that would have prevented this situation from ever occurring!

Apparently, Potiphar was too busy taking care of Pharaoh when he should have been taking care of his wife and her reputation! Potiphar's sin was, in reality, a sin of ignorance; whereas his wife's sin, was one of intent - the difference between commission and omission!

But, going back to our story! We find that the pride of Potiphar's wife simply would not allow her to take "NO" for an answer! Whoops, there it is! That old "pride of life" thing - the very same thing that caused Lucifer to fall from grace - pride will do it every time - it will lead to the "great fall" every single time! In Genesis 39:11-12 (NLT), we read: "One day, however, no one else was around when he was doing his work inside the house. (vs. 12) She came and grabbed him by his shirt, demanding, 'sleep with me!' Joseph tore himself away, but as he did, his shirt came off. She was left holding it as he ran from the house." There she was, holding the "tell-tale" shirt - her best-laid plans gone amuck! She had "set" the young man up, catching him by surprise, and leaving him with no alternative but to flee!

There he was, running through the courtyard, naked from the waist up, and there she was standing in her rage and fury! Perhaps this is what the Apostle Paul had in mind when he counseled his young preacher, Timothy, in 2 Timothy 2:22 (NLT): "Run from anything that stimulates youthful lust. Follow anything that makes you want to do right, pursue faith and love and peace, and enjoy the companionship of those who call on the Lord with pure hearts."

As we return to our story, we find these words, in Genesis 39:13-15 (NLT): "When she saw that she had his shirt and that he had fled, (vs. 14) she began screaming. Soon all the men around the place came running. 'My husband has brought this Hebrew slave here to insult us' she sobbed. 'He tried to rape me, but I screamed. (vs. 15) When he heard my loud cries, he ran and left his shirt behind with me.'" Excuse me! But, tell me, "Did anybody hear anyone scream in this story?" I certainly didn't, nor did these other men - however, they reasoned together that if the "Lady of the House" said she screamed, then, she did, in fact, scream! Perhaps, at one time or another, they too had been seduced by this bored, neglected woman - and, fearful of having her turn on them, decided to testify as witnesses for the plaintiff! More than likely, they figured that since she had his shirt in her hand, as proof, they could get away with giving false testimony!

In Proverbs 5:3-4 (NLT), we read: "The lips of an immoral woman are as sweet as honey, and her mouth is smoother than oil. (vs. 4) But the result is as bitter as poison, sharp as a double-edged sword." Perhaps, the wise ruler King Solomon had Potiphar's wife in mind when he wrote those words.

But, back to our story! In Genesis 39:19 (NLT), we read: "After hearing his wife's story, Potiphar was furious!" In effect, his wife was saying that all of this was Potiphar's fault - he was the one who brought this Hebrew slave into the household! Now, if that sounds familiar, it is! Do you remember when almighty God asked the first Adam, in the Garden of Eden, why he had eaten of the "forbidden fruit"? Adam told God, in response, that it was "that woman you gave me." Now, here was Potiphar's wife doing the same "blame-shifting" thing, saying to Potiphar, "that Hebrew slave you gave me." Adam did not succeed in his "pointing the finger at someone else" and neither did Potiphar's wife!

Now, look at this! Who was Potiphar furious with? The Holy Bible does not tell us; but, a reasonable person would infer that he was furious with his wife! Why do you say that, preacher? Another good question! Do you remember the law for adultery? If Potiphar had believed his wife, he would have had Joseph and his wife killed - the punishment was death! Yet, if we go to Genesis 39:20 (NLT), we read: "He took Joseph and threw him into the prison where the king's prisoners were held."

Continuing on to Genesis 39:21-23 (NLT), we discover these words: "But the Lord was with Joseph there, too, and he granted Joseph favor with the chief jailer. (vs. 22) Before long, the jailer put Joseph in charge of all the other prisoners and over everything that happened in the prison. (vs. 23) The chief jailer had no more worries after that, because Joseph took care of everything. The Lord was with him, making everything run smoothly and successfully."

In this story, we discover that Potiphar's wife committed seven (7) sins which almighty God finds abominable - what are they? It's in the Book, you can find it in Proverbs 6:17-19 (NLT): "haughty eyes, a lying tongue, hands that kill the innocent, (vs. 18) a heart that plots evil, feet that race to do wrong, (vs. 19) a false witness who pours out lies, a person who sows discord among brothers." Potiphar's wife was guilty as charged!

So, let's look at the final analysis of the events that took place in this story! My Bible tells me that almighty God was with Joseph everywhere - in the country and out of the country - in the house and out of the house - in the jail and out of the jail - almighty God was "omnipresent" in the life of Joseph! He was everywhere at once! In the eyes of almighty God, Joseph was locked up - but, he was not locked out! Almighty God did not forsake Joseph, nor will he forsake you or me! The writer of Hebrews, in Hebrews 13:5 (NLT), tells us: 'Stay away from the love of money; be satisfied with what you have. For God has said, 'I will never fail you. I will never forsake you.''

So, what about Potiphar's wife, what happened to her? Unfortunately, my Holy Bible does not tell me what happened to her - the Word simply leaves it to us to determine for ourselves! I believe that her punishment was far worse than Joseph's; because, I believe that she found herself imprisoned behind the prison bars of her own lust, her own revengeful attitude, and her own false testimony. I believe that her husband left her to her own devices - no longer trusting - no longer supportive! I believe that she was the forerunner to the "reprobate mind"!

Her most powerful weapon was the spirit of temptation, a spirit destroying marriages everyday second and causes more wives/husbands to feel un-wanted and sexy. If the spirit of temptation is existing in your marriage? Start destroying it today through prayer and repentance.

There's a story of a boy that One day a father said to his son, "Now, son, don't swim in that canal." "OK, Dad," he answered. But he came home carrying a wet bathing suit that evening. "Where have you been?" demanded the father. "Swimming in the canal," answered the boy. "Didn't I tell you not to swim there?" asked the father. "Yes, Sir," answered the boy. "Why did you?" he asked. "Well, Dad," he explained, "I had my bathing suit with me and I couldn't resist the temptation." "Why did you take your bathing suit with you?" he questioned. "So I'd be prepared to swim, in case I was tempted," he replied.

Many people I've their lives just like that. They expect to sin and so they live their lives in such a manner that they actually excite sin and make it easier for them to fall. Whenever we play with temptation, it is easy to drift into great danger. A woman was bathing in the Gulf of Mexico. She was enjoying the comfort of relaxing on an inflated cushion that kept her afloat. When she realized that she had been swept about a half mile out from the beach, she began to scream, but no one heard her. A coast guard craft found her five miles from the place where she first entered the water. She did not see her danger until she was beyond her own strength and ability.

The remedy for this is found in Romans 13:14, "*But put ye on the Lord Jesus Christ, and make not provision for the flesh, to fulfill the lusts thereof.*" Our text today speaks about a young man who faced a fearful time of temptation. Instead of falling, like so many do, Joseph weathered the storm of temptation and won a great victory in his spiritual life. He stayed clean in a situation where many others would have fallen.

The Character Of The Tempted - By watching Joseph and how he conducted himself during this attack, we can learn how we too can stand when temptation stalks us.

1. V. **8 He Met It With A Firm Refusal** - When the temptation came to him, Joseph was ready with a firm, "*No!*". The Bible doesn't say, but I am almost sure that Joseph had already settled this matter within his heart. He had already made the decision of what to do when temptation came. He had already decided that he would go with God and stay away from sin! When we allow our minds to be unprincipled and uncontrolled, we run the risk of being unprepared for the attacks of sin and Satan. When temptation comes after you, it is hard to say "*No!*", and mean it in the heat of the moment. But, if the decision has already been made, it is far easier to stand! That is why you have got to guard the mind and protect it from all the things that would enter it, pollute it and weaken your ability to mount a strong defense! (**Note**: I want to teach you one word that will help you in this matter of temptation. It is the word "*No!*". Learn it and use it! It will help you! Spurgeon said it like this: "*Learn to say no. It will be of more use to you than to be able to read Latin.*" This was the strategy Daniel and the 3 Hebrews boys adopted in Babylon and it worked like a charm. It still will!)

2. V. 8-9 **He Met It With A Faith-based Refusal** - First, Joseph refused on the grounds that Potiphar had placed Joseph in a position of power because he trusted him. He refused to violate that trust. However, at the very foundation of Joseph's refusal was his walk with His God. He knew that committing adultery with this woman might bring pleasure in the short term, but in the long term, it would mean violating the trust Potiphar had placed in him and it would cause a breach in his relationship with his God. And, even if Potiphar never found out, Joseph knew that God would know and he knew that Joseph would know. For Joseph, that was a price far too high to pay! His integrity before men, his walk with God and his ability to look into the mirror without guilt were worth more to Joseph than a few moments of physical pleasure! (**Note**: Before you give in to that temptation and do that thing that looks so enticing, take a moment to think about the consequences. What will happen to your testimony in the eyes of others when they find out? What will happen to your walk with the Lord? Will you be able to live with yourself?) (Note: For Joseph, the fear of the Lord was a powerful motivator! I realize that few people walk with that in their minds in our day. However, fearing God will keep you out of a lot of trouble! When you know that you will pay the price of chastisement, of being shelved and of a loss of fellowship with Him, it is worth saying "no" to a few temptations along life's way!)

3. V. 10 **He Met It With A Faithful Refusal** - Every day this woman tempted Joseph and every day he steadfastly refused her advances. He didn't resort to mind games like, "Well, if the Lord didn't want me to do this, He would just take it away from me." He just faithfully stood for the Lord and against the evil! (**Note**: We need to get this truth: Temptation is going to come and God is not likely to take it away! He will strengthen us and enable us to stand against it, but we are going to have to fight it and learn to take a stand! Not everything that you are offered in life is good for you. You need the wisdom of God to be able to choose that which is pleasing to him and to refrain from that which is not!) (**Note**: There is something very important to notice in **verse 10**. Joseph refused to listen to her words and he even refused to be with her. He came to the place where he physically avoided her! This is a great step in avoiding sinning through temptation. Don't flirt with it! Don't try to prove you can handle it! Never come to the place where you think you have it whipped! If something is a temptation to you, then avoid it like the plague! Don't be foolish enough to think that you can handle temptation and sin. They will show you short order that they can handle you, **1 Cor. 10:12**.) (Ill. On the TV show "Hee Haw," Doc Campbell is confronted by a patient who says he broke his arm in two places. The doc replies, "Well then, stay out of them places!")

4. V. 12 **He Met It With A Final Refusal** - When the big day came and this woman allowed her thoughts to find physical expression, she grabbed Joseph and said *"Lie with me!"* It was time to make a decision and he did! He spun out of that robe and ran out of the house, leaving her holding the garment! Joseph literally ran away from Potiphar's wife to preserve his character. (**Note**: You cannot have it both ways! You can either give into sin and pay the price for your pleasure, **Prov. 5:11-14**. Or, you can run from temptation and protect your testimony!) (Ill."What are you doing, son?" the shopkeeper asked a little boy whose eyes were on a large basket of apples outside the storefront. "Trying to steal one of those apples?" "No sir," replied the boy. "I'm trying not to.")

(**Note**: Before we leave this thought, I want to point out a few facts about temptation:

1. **Temptation is never from God** - **James 1:13** - Potiphar's wife tried to blame Joseph and Potiphar for her lust, **13-18**. Some people even try to blame God for their sins, but God is not responsible for the things that tempt you! God tests His children, but He always sets the test up so that we can pass. Satan tempts us, but always to make us fail! Temptation is never from God!

2. **Temptation is always from within** - **James 1:14-15** - Temptation always comes to us based on the things we already want. Just like a fisherman baits his hook with the proper bait to attract to the kind of fish he wishes to catch, Satan baits the hook of temptation with the very worm he knows we will like!

3. **Temptation Must Be Handled Properly - 1 Cor. 10:13** - God will make a way out of temptation, but we must be active in finding the door out! Here are a few suggestions for dealing with temptation:

a. **Deal with it Immediately** - Don't allow it to linger in your life and grow out of control. As Barney Fife would have said it, "Nip it in the bud!" Get before God and ask for His help!

b. **Deal with it Realistically** - Understand that sin is more powerful than you are. It will destroy you if it has an opportunity. Do not give it that chance! Jesus said this ti His disciples, ***"Watch and pray, that ye enter not into temptation: the spirit indeed is willing, but the flesh is weak."***, **Matt. 26:41**.

c. **Deal with it Ruthlessly** - Whatever you have to do to avoid the temptation is in order! Remember what Jesus said about this matter - **Mark 9:43-48**. Regardless of what you have to do, get away from it! (Ill. During the Falkland's War England's Prime Minister, Margaret Thatcher, ordered the bombing of the British airstrips in Port Stanley to prevent them from being used by the enemy!) (Ill. Logger with his foot caught in a long wooden shoot!)

d. **Deal with it Consistently** - Learn to be consistent in your resistance. If you aren't, you will be caught off guard and overcome! (Ill. The same wind can send one ship east and another west. Which way the ship goes is determined by the set of the sails!)

e. **Deal with it Confidently** - We have the Lord's great promise in **1 Cor. 10:13**. God will make a way of escape, just be sure you look for it! Most of give into temptation, not because we can't get out of it, but because we don't want out of it!

III. V. 20-23 **THE TRIUMPH JOSEPH EXPERIENCED**

(Ill. I will be brief here, but I want you to know that Joseph benefitted from his stand against temptation and sin. Let me point out three ways in which this is true.)

A. V. 21, 23 **He Triumphed In His Relationship With The Savior** - Notice how the Bible says that the Lord continues to be with Joseph and to bless his life. Those who stay true to the Lord can be assured of His smile upon them and upon all they do. Those who stray from the path of righteousness will find themselves alienated from God and from His blessings in their lives. This is worth far more than any pleasure sin might offer! (Ill. This was Paul's fear - **1 Cor. 9:27**)

B. V. 20-23 **He Triumphed In His Relationship With His Own Self** - Joseph's integrity was intact. His reputation in Potiphar's house had been undermined, but his character remained intact! He had successfully weathered the storm of temptation and he had retained the ability to look into the mirror without guilt! Friends, that are worth more than anything sin can offer you!

C. V. 22-23 **He Triumphed In His Relationship With Sovereignty** - It may look like all Joseph got for his refusal of this woman was trouble. After all, he was thrown into prison. However, because he stayed true to the Lord, he was still in the center of God's will for his life, even though it may not have appeared so on the surface. Before many years could pass, Joseph would be raised up by the power of God and would sit as second in command to Pharaoh. The best you can do is stay close to God, live holy and trust Him to being His best into your life in His time. Getting God's best is always worth more than what sin can give!

- Men who trap animals in Africa for zoos in America say that one of the hardest animals to catch is the ring-tailed monkey. For the Zulus of that continent, however, it's simple. They've been catching this agile little animal with ease for years. The method the Zulus use is based on knowledge of the animal. Their trap is nothing more than a melon growing on a vine. The seeds of this melon are a favorite of the monkey. Knowing this, the Zulus simply cut a hole in the melon, just large enough for the monkey to insert his hand to reach the seeds inside. The monkey will stick his hand in, grab as many seeds as he can, then start to withdraw it. This he cannot do. His fist is now larger than the hole. The monkey will pull and tug, screech and fight the melon for hours. But he can't get free of the trap unless he gives up the seeds, which he refuses to do. Meanwhile, the Zulus sneak up and nab him.

Chapter 16

"Destroying the spirit of temptation on the mind"

Hebrews 13:4

Marriage is to be held in honor among all, and the marriage bed is to be undefiled; for fornicators and adulterers God will judge.

Before we can destroy the spirit of temptation we must first expose the reason this spirit occurs in our lives/marriages and often times leading to affairs.

REASONS FOR AN AFFAIR

Everyone on this earth desires 1 thing in life and that is we want to feel good about ourselves, and if for some reason you don't feel that way, you may seek/find it in and from another person. A lover will only make you feel good about yourself for a short time; don't destroy your marriage over lustful time of feeling good.

A lover often gives a person the courage to do something he or she couldn't do alone, which is to seek a divorce.

No one gets married intending to have an affair. Once involved, emotions of lust start to flow and excitement kicks and they know that it's not right but they believe they can keep the affair in the smallest area of their life and in some cases their heart. A person may feel they are not hurting anyone but are hurting more than just their spouse especially if there are children involved. An affair often enables the person to be more sexually adventurous and to express their sexuality - in ways not done with their spouse. The results are very destructive.

The Primary Reasons for an Affair

1. Excitement

2. Romantic Love

3. Sex

4. Mid-life Crisis

5. Anger

6. Escape

7. Loneliness

8. Obsession

9. Soul mate

10. Lesbian/Gay Orientation

In breaking these reasons down, here is what I've found.

1.) **Excitement**- Affairs become exciting solely because it is filling the excitement you're desiring/missing in your marriage. Intense eye contact, soft slow kisses, sexual touches of the body, secret meetings filled with excitement and the thrill of getting caught. In most cases the lack of excitement can be easily targeted and fixed in a marriage and that reason is normally because a routine has set in the marriage such as: work, being too predictable, tiredness from life itself, no vacations for just the two of you to rekindle your fires and rather than make the vacation happen, an affair happens because the affair brings the excitement and the person feels more alive than they ever have been because they're getting the attention they've been crying out for.

2.) **Romance Love-** Romance is all women really desire in love, it's what they call sex to them, holding them, flowers on none special days. Dinner dates in romantic places that are not the norm, unexpected messages/voicemails, lunch dates, being told how cute her new hairstyle is, listening to her talk without interrupting her, holding hands while walking the canal or river bank, eating at the same dinner table over candle lights and once she doesn't get these things in her marriage she turns to the affair that will provide all of these things.

3.) **Sex-** Sex is very imperative in a marriage and it seems to die with each passing second in a marriage which causes married couples to become disconnected, not only physically but there is a spiritual connection behind a married couple having sex that gives them a deeper connection to each other. Married couples on average are having sex once maybe twice a month and in some cases it is far worse than that and this is what gives the enemy free right to invoke the spirit of temptation in your marriage and his job won't be very hard because the need is already there.

4.) **Midlife crisis-** This comes when your spouse feels there is no excitement in the marriage anymore and they desire to go out and create some excitement and in doing so, most never go out with the intention of having sexual intercourse with someone else, most go out to flirt just to see if they still got it and the flirt turns into more than they expected but they found the spark to a new life they've been yearning for that is absent from the marriage. Once this spark has been lit, it then turns into a massive fire that becomes hard to put out because your spouse now feels as if they're living, being loved, held and appreciated for the first time in years.

5.) **Anger-** This spirit destroys everything in its path, it's selfish and it becomes angrier when you don't entertain the desires it wants. Anger can arise in a marriage for many reasons such as money, never keep any form of money secret, it can come back to hurt your marriage in the long run, secrecy creates an atmosphere for lack of trust. Anger can arise when someone is unhappy in the marriage, when hurt/pain is still there from infidelity, one doing all the heavy lifting in the marriage while the other just sleeps and chills with their friends all the time, gambling addictions, drug addictions, children's mother that are not respectful of your household, In-laws not respecting your space and marriage, selfishness, feeling un-wanted/needed. Any of these and so much more can cause a person to get involved in an affair based on how they feel or think they're being treated in a marriage and will cause an argument just to leave the house to be with the person they feel appreciates them.

6.) **Escape-** This is that person that just wants to get away from it all. They don't feel comfortable in their own home, they don't feel loved in their own home, this is that person that becomes depressed at the thought of going home because they're tired of all the pain they feel when in the home, the routine in the home, the lack of love making in the home, the lack of communication in the home, the hidden secrets in the home, the issues that were never addressed before marriage, the way the home makes them feel like they're in a prison, the regret of getting married but now there are children involved, so instead of leaving you just want to get away, even if it's just for a day but getting away in this feelings causes one to get away into another person's arms and bed. Address these feelings with your spouse, cheating is never worth it.

Marriage of Pearls

Many marriages/relationships are destroyed because of false allegations against the marriage that are spoken out of jealousy and envy for what God has given you both and the enemy at all cost will pound these false words into your minds and as long as you both are on the same page and are rejecting these allegations, they cannot penetrate your marriage. It is only when one of you start to believe these allegations that gives the enemy full authority to no enter into your home and marriage and dwell there in on every single lie and even creating more through the imagination of the spouse and the enemy is now operating in full deception in your marriage with the instructions to destroy it by any means.

For instance, your marriage is going great, you both are happy, in love and all of sudden one spouse comes with questions out of no more through the spirit of insecurity and suspicions questioning the other spouse's loyalty and commitment to the marriage and to them. Discern that this is the work of the devil to cause a spirit of divination to enter into the marriage and destroy any confidence they had in the marriage.

The spouse knows in their heart that this is a trick of the enemy and knows that the marriage is the best it's ever been and instead of denouncing these thoughts they entertain them and the enemy begins to laugh and pound even harder into the mind of the spouse and plants seeds of doubt.

- "Your spouse doesn't love you!"

- "Your spouse is cheating with someone they work with!"

- "Your marriage will fail!"

- "Search they're phone and social media messages!"

- "See, they were talking too long to that woman/man!"

- "Why do you think you only make love once or twice a month?"

- "They're too good for a person like you!"

- "You're doing all the work!" "Just leave!"

- "They don't even touch you the same!"

- "You deserve better!"

If we look at this in the flesh we'll continue to entertain these lies and the door to your marriage remains open for the enemy to come in even deeper and continue his plan of destruction on your marriage and family, preying on your now unstable emotions and newly invoked fear of losing your spouse and family that you've always said you'd fight and die for, but the issue now is that yes, you are dying but you're not putting up much of a fight because you're entertaining things that you know to be false. Once the enemy has penetrated your mind into the depths of your soul, he'll use the worrying that you now have as a tool to get you to buy in a 100% to the false allegations on your marriage and will use you as the instrument to bring the false allegations into reality in your marriage.

This brings in the spirit of confusion and new mind games are now in play in your marriage and your perception of the smallest things in your marriage will become the biggest, bent, twisted explosions creating an hostile environment for your marriage and every second is controlled by a ticking time bomb and if not deactivated soon it then only becomes a matter of time before the death of your marriage is reality.

Yes, this is a form of temptation, temptation to make you think differently than what you normally do. When you embrace the tricks and mind games of the enemy, you have now given them all power over you and your situation and these types of mind games and easily become lustful thoughts to make you step outside of your marriage based on the falseness that has been placed inside of your mind. These lies and false allegations are meant to destroy you, causing you to become sick from the worrying and stress and even make you have nervous breakdowns and if this is you, beseech you to take totally control over your mind today and begin to speak God's word over your mind and life to destroy the lies of the enemy because the process of destruction will continue to work in your life until you break free from the lies of the enemy.

Deception leading to temptation only occurs in a marriage when a person embraces the lies of the enemy and once embraced that gives the lies all the power it needs to become a reality into the marriage and begin its deception leading into temptations.

We must understand that we have spiritual authority over every temptation spirit of the devil, every trick of the devil, every device of the devil that he has set to destroy us and once we believe that we can then defeat these thoughts that are sent to penetrate our minds and we must not be ignorant of Satan's devices that are against us.

II Corinthians 2:11, Paul gives us a clue as to what the main road the devil will use to try and destroy us. Paul writes, "We are not ignorant of Satan devices." But the sad truth is that in this day and age we are ignorant of his devices because we have raised up a generation of carnal Christians that instead of love for God they are in love with Hip Hop, in love with the Coco and everything designed today is designed to destroy the human mind and cause us to think less and become more dependent on out T.V's and phones, that is why you see families out to eat and everyone is on their cell phones, there is no more intimacy at the dinner table, this is a trick of the devil to get your mind into playing his games.

The word devices in this text describes the attacks that Paul faced and resisted, so that we know that even Paul had to deal with mental assaults from the enemy and we must know that we can make anything we want good or bad just by thinking and the bible even tells us that if you think a thing, it is so. Our thoughts/mind is the enemies number source, just look at all the issues you've had in your marriage/relationship so far and you will see that 99% of them started in your mind and you lost control over every thought you had, every emotion that you had and we must not give Satan that kind of power over our lives. Stop listening to yourself regarding things in your marriage and start speaking to yourself about the goodness of God in your marriage.

You must break the generational curse off your family dealing with broken, unhappy marriages by keeping God at the center of yours. Just because your parents marriage didn't work doesn't mean that yours won't work. Your marriage is just that, yours to see if succeeds or fails.

If your marriage is in trouble and you both desire your marriage to get well. Turn it over to God and in an instant your marriage shall be fixed. You must cast down all imaginations that the enemy has planted in your mind about you, your marriage, your life and stop taking advice from people that are either single or their marriage is broken, that becomes the blind leading the blind and your marriage must seek out spiritual guidance from someone with the anointing to help you heal your marriage through prayer and the power of Jesus Christ.

There are powers, principalities, rulers of darkness and spiritual wickedness in high places that seeks to destroy your marriage and we must crucify our flesh in marriage to discern when the enemy is upon our marriage. These evil forces are working none stop behind the scenes in your life seeking to control, manipulate your flesh and mind. That's why you wake up tired, wake up with headaches, body aches, mental aches and many other problems because you've been fighting in yourself. Yes, your body rested but your mind was in a fight with these rulers of darkness that were planting seeds in your mind about your marriage.

Marriage of Pearls

At some point in your marriage, it will come face to face with evil forces that desire to come against it and the questions you need to ask your marriage today is "Are we ready for a battle?" "Can our marriage survive the battle?" If you can't answer those two questions, I suggest that you get your marriage deeply planted in God. Because when Paul says ruler of darkness that comes from the word kratos which means to have raw power. Not just any kind of raw power, but power that has an order to it and has specific reasons for its creation and the reason was to destroy the mind of the children of God.

Both of you must take a stand against the wiles of the enemy and understand that you are to stand strong together in the eyes of conflict and to do this your marriage must have on the whole armor of God, so that you are able to stand against the wiles of the devil Ephesians 6:11.

You must understand this because this puts your marriage in spiritual warfare not physical warfare. It is impossible to have a healthy balanced marriage without having God as the head of the marriage and you both being prepared for the spiritual attacks that will come upon your marriage. God is telling us with this word wiles exactly how the devil operates and how he will come to attack our minds to destroy not only our marriages but to destroy our lives.

The word wiles is translated to carry the idea of something cunning, crafty, subtle, or even full of trickery. But, the most meaning for this word is road. This tells us that the devil has created a road of trickery but the good thing is that it's only one road and not multiple roads, so the enemy comes with the same tricks every time he attacks you. However, he has become a master artist of this one trick and does it very well. In a marriage that road of trickery is temptation and the reason we must guard not only our minds against the words of the enemy but guard our eyes from seeing lustful things that may cause us sin and not know it. The bible says that if you lust with your eyes you have committed adultery.

If you continue to see the same pattern in your marriage that hasn't been there that has become unhealthy, causing arguments and lack of trust, address these things in prayer because the enemy is hard at work and we will never see these things with fleshly eyes and the longer these things are not addressed the more powerful and deeper the enemy gets and he command is to not stop until your marriage has been utterly destroyed and there is nothing left of it with no hopes of repairing the marriage after separation or divorce.

For your marriage to survive the wiles/devices of the devil, you must make a mental decision and charge your minds to "bring into captivity every thought to the obedience of Christ." It is dangerous to listen to others about our marriage and in most cases we're only giving the enemy ammunition to fire back and destroy us when we place our marital issues into the hands of those operating for Satan and they don't have a clue that they are working in evil spirits because they themselves have laid down and slept with the demon and have become one with him.

The enemy attacks the mind because whoever controls the mind controls, the body, the soul, health, the tongue and the emotions of a person. Don't think for a second the devil doesn't know this, his first trick on this road was deceiving the mind of Eve in the Garden of Eden to destroy the first marriage in God and he seeks to do the same to your marriage through penetrating your intellect so that he may plant seeds of falsehood and deception with a trigger of destruction. Once this stage is completed the devil can then begin to invite the spirit of manipulation into your mind and marriage and bring you and your marriage into spiritual captivity. This spirit of manipulation must be destroyed by the power of God and you must be renewed in your mind through God and the word of God. If you are not renewed in your mind you will be giving the devil power over your thinking, your emotions, your soul, and your overall life as you know it.

For assuredly, I say to you, whoever says to this mountain. "Be removed and cast into the sea." And does not doubt in his heart, but believes that those things he says will come to pass; he will have whatever he says. Therefore I say to you, whatever things you ask when you pray, believe that you receive them, and you will have them. Mark 11:23-24

Whatever is in the face of your marriage you can destroy it right now!!! What is it!?!? Is it Unemployment? Lust, Perversion, Control, Adultery, Communication, Finances, trust, undefeated sin from the past? Whatever it is, the power lies in you to speak to it and say, "BE THOU REMOVED!"

Speak to that mountain in your marriage and tell it to be removed right now in the name of Jesus!!!!

A Prayer for a renewed marriage.

God we thank and we praise you for all that you have done in this marriage, for the years you've provided for us, for the storms you've brought us through, the times where everyone else counted us out but you remained faithful in blessing us. God WE come against every device of the devil, everyone mind trickery he may have planted in our marriage, every curse and false allegations WE destroy in the might name of Jesus!!! WE rebuke our own families that are being used by the devil and WE rebuke the seed of destruction they desire to plant in Jesus mighty name!!! WE kneel before you together seeking your power to lift us up our of the pit of lions and bring us into your court and WE promise to enter with thanksgiving and praise on

our lips for all that you have done!!! God please teach us forgiveness so that we can truly move forward in you Lord and please forgive us for any wrong we may have done in your sight. In Jesus name AMEN!!!

Chapter 17

Putting the armor of God on your marriage.

Ephesians 6:11 "Put on the whole armor of God, that ye maybe able to stand against the wiles of the devil."

It is very imperative that your marriage has on the whole armor of God and so do you!

- **Loin belt of truth-** this the written word of God! This is the most important piece weapon that we have at our disposal as it is the only weapon that has gone from the spiritual into the physical realm for us to use. The Roman soldiers wore loin belts to hold all of their weapons in place and if this was not in place everything would fall apart. Likewise, if this weapon is not in your marriage, regardless of what you do to hold it and keep it together, it soon just fall apart. You must not ignore the word of God and you must not cease to apply it to your life/marriage on a daily basis, because if you do, you will have freely chosen to the enemy not only destroy your whole spiritual man/woman but you have chosen to let him destroy your marriage.

Your marriage can not function in the realm God intended for it to if the word of God is not in place in your marriage. Your marriage may get through a few storms and years but it will soon run out of love, desire, emotions, hugs, kisses and of-course the intercourse by now is dead and thoughts of an affair have taken place in your minds and it will only be a matter of time when you start to fall to pieces spiritually and lose more trust in God. A very powerful and vicious demonic assault will take action on your marriage and the barrier that God had in place will be broken through and all hell will consume your marriage.

If you desire your marriage to make until death do you part, you must begin to put the word of God in it!!! RIGHT NOW!!! NOT LATER!!! Allow it to be the loin belt that holds your marriage together!!! The word of God "Bible" must be the final deciding factor in your marriage, not your friends, not your family members and not even you…

- **Breast plate of righteousness-** When a marriage knows that God is the foundation and center of the marriage and the breast plate of righteousness is firmly in place- it doesn't matter what how many shots are fired at your marriage, how many arrows are thrown your way because not one shot or arrow will prosper against your marriage. No false allegations shall prosper, no evil thoughts will be able to penetrate your mind when the breast plate of righteousness is in place in your marriage.

However, it seems that 70% of marriages are walking in hurt, pain, anger, divorce, walking with their heads down; shoulders are no longer standing up straight in the confident position. The enemy has manipulated and victimized these marriages, so much so that they no longer pray together or even go to church together. He has convinced many that their marriage is not worth fighting for. But the scripture in verse 14 tells us to "stand, throw your shoulders back hold your head up high, and walk tall and confident, as all proud and victorious solders do!"

The enemy will try to slander and destroy your marriage but before you run out to defend your marriage make sure your breast plate is

Marriage of Pearls

firmly locked in the lord, don't allow the enemy to convince you that your marriage won't work and that there is no reason to talk it out with your spouse because they won't listen to you. Those are all lies of the enemy to impart a spirit of divorce and that is why it's imperative that you and your spouse know God for yourselves and know that when you have the breast plate active in your marriage everything will change for the better.

- **Shoes of Peace-** Wearing shoes of peace in your marriage can be one of the greatest weapons you could have. Peace not only protects your marriage, but it also gives you a very strong and brutal weapon to use against the enemy when he attacks your marriage. If this piece of armor is used the right way, it will keep all those against you and your marriage even the spiritual demons will be kept where they belong. One massive kick with these shoes and the enemy and his plan to destroy you will be destroyed on contact!

The brass on these shoes allowed the solider to walk through some of the rockiest places and never get hurt and because of the massive protective greaves on these shoes, the enemy could kick as hard as he desired but the soldier would never get hurt or have broken legs. Likewise, the enemy can kick at your marriage as hard as they desire but with the protection God has put in place in your marriage through this weapon, no part of your marriage shall be broken, destroyed or injured! When you marriage is walking in the peace of God, it is then protected from all tricks of the enemy in his attempts to destroy your marriage.

Peace is a very powerful divine weapon that will rise up a shield of protection from the vicious attacks that have been planned against your marriage. This weapon of peace from and of God will keep the enemy confused when he comes against you as God will guard your heart and mind against all the wiles of the enemy. The peace of God that passes all understanding is KEEPING the peace in your marriage, allow it to stay there!!!

Speak Romans 16:20 over your marriage every night. "And the God of peace shall bruise Satan under your feet shortly."

Watch God give you the victory over your marriage, over your finances, over your children, over your miracles and all things you desire!!!

- **The Shield of Faith-** The shield of faith is the way of escape for your marriage from the fiery darts and arrows shot at your marriage because when your faith is activated and in-front of you every temptation that the enemy tries will be quenched in the name of Jesus!!!

Remember that the Roman soldiers shield of faith was made of leather and it had to be maintained for it to be effective in battle and if not maintained correctly over a period of time the leather wouldn't function at its full potential and once put under pressure in battle, it would crack and fall into pieces on the battle ground before you. The result of not maintaining your Shield of faith is death. Death to every are of your marriage, death to your finances, death to your health, death to your relationship with your children, death to your spirit, death to your mind and death will overtake you until your physical man is dead!!! Just like the Roman who desired to live and win the battle, it was very imperative that he used the oil to vial and apply it to his shield and just like this soldier you must do the same thing with your marriage and apply the oil of God to it, keep it well maintained so that when your marriage is put to the test it doesn't crack under pressure and to ensure this, your Shield of Faith will require frequent anointings of the holy Spirit. Without this frequent touch of the Holy Spirit the power in your marriage will become dead, hard to maintain, stiff, and it will break in combat! The issues of lack of faith In your marriage can no longer go unaddressed and never seeking God's will for your marriage as to STOP!!! Without God's spirit in you and your marriage it will be very hard to stand and fight of the spirits that put your marriage to the test and under demonic attack. Any cracks in your faith will give the enemy access to kill and destroy!!!

That is why God tells us to "CAST DOWN Imaginations, and every high thing that exalted itself against the knowledge of God." (II Corinthians 10:5). Think about it for a minute, how much destruction can the enemy do if your faith has already cast down the imagination? That's what the Shield of Faith does, it destroys all allegations and any hell the devil tried to bring on your marriage and places them under your feet! Your marriage may have endured to strikes from the enemy in the past but that was only because your faith wasn't out in-front of your marriage and now that it is, we can stand strong in the face of the enemy with our Shield of Faith and say "WE WIN!!!"

Make sure that after today your marriage is fully equipped with the Shield of Faith and that it is well maintained with the oil and Holy Spirit of God and walk in your new faith and I promise you that the enemy will not be able to penetrate your marriage, your mind, your finances, your emotions, your health, or any part of your lives!!!

- **Helmet of salvation-** To protect us from manipulation, disease and attacks from the enemy, God has provided to us a helmet of salivation and we must find out what the salvation of our marriage means from the inside and out, even calling the deep things in our marriage into order with God's will for our marriage. Once you have the knowledge of your salvation and the salvation of your marriage, if won't even matter what tricks the devil will try and use against you!!!

We will stand on the death, burial and resurrection of Christ and know that our lives and marriage was purchased with the blood of Christ and with this knowledge the enemy won't be able to penetrate our helmet of salvation.

Ephesians 6 calls this our defensive weapon, a weapon to protect our minds from the attacks, tricks and allegations of the enemy. Satan does this so that he can attempt to rob you from your blessings from God by getting you to think your way of trusting God's word and removing your faith through fear and worry and steal any joy that you may have left in your marriage so that he can then go in for the kill from the inside and instead of birthing greatness, the enemy desires that you birth destruction and evil spirits, that way he can any and every good thing from you that he can. Must fill the mind of our marriage with all that God has done for the marriage and we must mediate faithfully on the word of God daily so that we may protect the mind of our marriage and allow the word of God to work in us and in our marriage and through the word of God everything shall be renewed through the power of God.

The questionable areas in your marriage the enemy used to use an area of attack on a daily basis will no longer be attackable because now your marriage has the Helmet of salvation firmly in place and the Holy Spirit will now encompass your marriage both mentally and emotionally through the power of the death, burial and resurrection of Christ…

- **Sword of The Spirit-** "The Sword of The Spirit is the word of God" says Apostle Paul. "Word" in the Greek in this text is from the Greek word rhema, which is a very familiar Greek word used in the New Testament. It is something very vividly spoken, unquestionable and unmistakable. A word from the Lord that comes quickly that the Holy Spirit Supernaturally drops in your mind and impart special powers into the mind of the believer giving them direction.

Marriage of Pearls

This weapon is so important because when the word of God gets in your heart and mind, that very word begins to impart wisdom, knowledge, understanding and most of light and direction from God. It doesn't matter how hopeless your marriage looks right now, God has a sword that he is waiting and ready to rise up in your situation with a specific divine word of guidance to deliver your marriage from the stronghold of the enemy. This word can only be produced to your marriage through prayer and reading of the word of God and when this sword comes up from the spirit of your marriage it will show you what you need to do and where to go.

The devil will ramp up his allegations and lies against your marriage the moment your sword is about to be produced in your marriage but everything at this point will fail because the light your sword produces will push back all darkness that is upon your marriage because it will destroy like a mighty blade coming out of your mouth and the amount of power that comes from the mouth of your marriage is based upon the amount of word that is in your marriage, little word equals little power, much word equals much power and to receive these rhema words from God in your marriage you must make the written word of God, the centerpiece of your marriage.

So, now is the time to stand in the face of the devil and refuse to allow him to destroy your marriage any longer, refuse to feel lonely any longer, refuse to let your home feel like a prison any longer, refuse to be mistreated any longer, refuse to let the love your life fall, refuse to let the enemy be victorious over your marriage. You have the power to speak to the demonic presence in your marriage right now and destroy it by using that power that the Holy Spirit has welded up in you and in your marriage and let those faith words fill your mouth and when the enemy sees your power and sees that you're no longer intimidated he will flee from you, your spouse and your marriage!!!

Chapter 18

The Importance of Marital Sex!!!

First we must ask ourselves, "why is sex some important in a marriage?" Let us also understand that **sex is not just a functional "chore" that we do because we feel obligated to do it**, instead we must see sex as a **"spiritual connection"** to our spouse that draws us into a world of becoming one with them on a level/dimension that God created for martial sex to take place but in today's world, sex has taken a back seat in marriages across the world, thus causing the spirit of pornography to enter into your marriage and there are more women masturbating to porn today than ever before, it has become a daily routine them to masturbate to porn instead of making love to their spouse.

"Therefore shall a man leave his father and his mother, and shall cleave unto his wife: and they shall be one flesh" (**Genesis 2:24 KJV**). Other translations render "leave and cleave" as "leave and be united" (NIV), "leave and be joined" (NASB), and "leave and hold fast"

It is very clear in this scripture that God is talking about marital intimacy, he also stated that two shall become one flesh, setting the spiritual platform for marital intimacy through the word "cleave" as this word means to join with, adhere and creates a spiritual joining of two people into one entity. This also means that you don't leave your spouse when sex has taken the back seat in your, instead, you find ways to rekindle that fire that has been covered up by the dust of working, parenting, schooling, stress, frustration and in most cases depression, once you tackle the root cause, then you can begin to get your sex life back in your marriage to the forefront of your marriage. If for any reason, either spouse refuses to leave and cleave, problems will begin to rise in your marriage life never before, thus further destroying any possibility to rekindle the fire in your marriage.

Sex is the Gorilla glue that uniquely and spiritually bonds a husband and wife together as one. We take this part of our marriage for granted and that it is taken for granted the more your marriage is falling to the pits of hell right into the hands of Satan and he will use this as a tool to manipulate your mind and will begin to place lustful thoughts in your mind while you're awake and while you are sleeping and you will find yourself lustfully and fleshly aroused with no plans or thoughts of wanting your spouse instead you're lusting after something or someone else throughout your day and the this lust plays a major role on your job and this lust will have you fall into temptations with someone you've never look at in this way before but since the enemy has planted the seed of lust in your mind, this seed has started to produce it's fruits using you as the root in which it is to grow. We must not neglect the needs of our spouses as the Apostle Paul stated. Because in neglected their sexual needs we place a stronghold on our marriage that is very difficult to remove without the power of God. Let's look at what Apostle Paul says.

- *1 Corinthians 7:3-5:*

Marriage of Pearls

The wife's body does not belong to her alone but also to her husband. In the same way, the husband's body does not belong to him alone but also to his wife. Do not deprive each other except by mutual consent and for a time, so that you may devote yourselves to prayer. Then come together again so that Satan will not tempt you because of your lack of self-control.

We have a God given obligation to seek out ways to satisfy our spouses sexually even when we don't feel like it and remember this is not a "chore" this is far from "washing dishes" or "spring cleaning" this is a command from God that we're to literally become one flesh!!! This command is not to be taken lightly as most couples do, they have sex all the time before marriage and once they get married sex happens once a month if you're lucky and this shouldn't ever happen in a marriage but the sad truth is IT DOES and IT MUST BE DETROYED!!! As this is called sexual witchcraft, seduction to get what you want and once you have it you turn it off like a light switch that never had a bulb in it and that is the reason the marriage lacks sexual intimacy because through this form of witchcraft the wrong spirit was placed in the relationship and there was never the spirit of God placed in it thus leaving intimacy out and giving you just sex with no real feelings or emotions because if there was true love and emotions involved, you'd have to fight each other off when it came to sexual intimacy. Expectations should always be set before marriage on the amount of sex/lack thereof the marriage will have.

- ## Here are a few reasons why sex is so important in a marriage:

1.) **Stress reliever-** Sex has been proven to remove stress from our bodies because when we have sex it produces happy hormones in our bodies and it is a scientific fact that couples who have a lot of sex have less stress than does that don't. So, what do you have to lose? Plan your romantic nights now and rekindle that fire in your marriage and I promise, all that stress that just sitting on your shoulders and mind will be destroyed instantly!!!

2.) **Causes Emotional Healing**- Sex is more than a physical act with your spouse sex will always start with romance and end with romance and this act is what cause couples to cuddle and hold each other after the act of sex has taken place and those couples that have sex and cuddle afterwards demonstrate more emotional feelings in the marriage than those that don't because they feel the need to kiss, hug, touch more often and they tend to have no problem with demonstrating this in public our around friends and family. This is because sex makes our body produce more oxytocin, this is a hormone that makes us feel the need to love and trust somebody.

3.) **Balancing the female hormones**- A night full of sexual passion can do much more than just satisfying your wife and having her ready to make breakfast in the morning. Your wife being more sexually active produces what is called estrogen and when a woman's body stops producing this her body begins to tear down in many ways but actively having sex at least once a week can delay menopause, regulate your monthly cycle and increase your fertility and these are just a few of the perks for women to have sex at least once a week in your marriage.

4.) **Cancer risk reduced**- Having sex has been proven to reduce the risk of prostate cancer and breast cancer. So, fight the good fight and engage in some great sexual activities with your spouse right NOW!!! Yes, drop this book and go surprise your spouse with some love making!!!!

5.) **Helps you live longer-** Sex rejuvenates, heals wounds, and makes you more flexible and less prone to various illnesses. It works as a metabolism and immunity booster, it reduces the risk of a stroke and it also fights the aging process! Add that positive, happy, sexy feeling and you'll stay young forever stress free!!!

6.) <u>I want more NOW!!!</u>- The more you engage in sex with your spouse the more you will want sex because having sexual intimacy will increase your libido and you'll think about sex more and need it more often than before.

The flesh is very powerful and uses that as a major tool to make us become one, however, we are to do our part as well to become one and stay as one and build a oneness into our marriages. (Remember Matt. 19:3-12) that says we are to BECOME "one flesh" meaning that part of that is our sexual relationships that are to make us one, but in God's eyes it is more than just sex and to most women today it is more than just sex in their eyes and women that have lost their desire to have sex with their spouse have lost what God created as a main ingredient in making us one, "Intimacy" yes, intimacy is very important between a husband and wife and this intimacy is more than sexual, we are to intimate **physically, spiritually, and emotionally.** To further understand those actions we are to take, let's break them down.

Physically Intimacy- is sensual **proximity** or touching. It is an act or reaction, such as an expression of **feelings** (including close **friendship, love**, or **sexual attraction**), between people. Examples of physical intimacy include being inside someone's **personal space, holding hands, hugging, kissing, caressing**, and **sexual activity**.

It is possible to be physically intimate with someone without actually touching them; however, a certain **proximity** is necessary. For instance, a sustained **eye contact** is considered a form of physical intimacy, analogous to touching. When a person enters someone else's **personal space** for the purpose of being intimate, it is physical intimacy, regardless of the lack of actual physical contact.

Most people partake in physical intimacy, which is a natural part of interpersonal relationships and **human sexuality**, and research has shown it has health benefits. A hug or touch can result in the release of **oxytocin, dopamine**, and **serotonin**, and in a reduction in stress **hormones**. Notice all the verbs that must take place even for us to have physically intimacy. Take a moment and be the Doctor of your marriage and see if all of these verbs are being applied to your marriage and if there is even one missing, take ACTION TODAY to put it back in your marriage as the first step in repairing the breach of your marriage. There must a level of chemistry that is created through this very first step that instantly draws you to your spouse as it did in the beginning when you first met and at times you both had so much chemistry through "physical Intimacy" that you often felt like you were the only two in a room full of people and as if you were dancing in the clouds while the cool breeze from the midnight sky brushed against you both, drawing you closer to each other.

- **Spiritual Intimacy-** This level of your marriage can only happen when you and your spouse surrender your lives, marriage, children and complete house over to God. This level is not going to be obtained by everyone, this level will only be obtained by those that have a personal relationship with God through our Lord Jesus Christ. To again look at your marriage to see if you have a spiritual relationship, look to see if you are currently struggling with any of the following:

1. You are experiencing a high level of conflict in many areas. Areas that were not a problem either before you

got married or before one of you turned your life over to Christ.

2. There are times you are sitting in your bed, at work or even driving to work asking God, **"Is this really my life?" "Why do I feel so incomplete/lost/rejected?"**

3. Your marriage seems to lack any type of foundation and even a promising commitment.

4. There are no more boundaries for even guarding your marriage and no one seems to care if the marriage lives or dies anymore.

5. You both walk around the house in silence and at times you feel like a prisoner in your own house.

6. If you find yourself saying I love my spouse but I am no longer in love with my spouse.

7. Infidelity continues to happen in your marriage and all the trust you had for your spouse is now gone.

8. You start to feel "less sexy, less intelligent, less wanted, less loved" or lesser in any part of your marriage or life. This one is a sign of **"Manipulation"** We'll talk more about that later in the book.

Please understand that spiritual growth must be obtained and **BE** the responsibility of both the husband and the wife. You both have to desire to have a closer relationship with God and agree together that we will bring ourselves continually into the presence of God. Physically Intimacy sets the platform for your marriage to takeoff and spiritual Intimacy becomes the afterburners that causes your marriage to take flight in the spirit realm. Spiritual connection is what keeps you together in your marriage through the power of God. Here are just a few of the benefits for allowing God to lead your marriage in spiritual Intimacy:

1. It empowers you to celebrate the love you have for each other as well as appreciate the strength you both share for each other.
2. It empowers you to connect to each other on a deeper level.
3. It empowers you to connect with God as he reveals the purpose and plan for your marriage.
4. It empowers you to bless and love each other with God's love.
5. It empowers you to bring your deepest values and desires into agreement with each other.
6. It empowers you to open the doors to the deepest levels of communication.
7. It empowers your marriage to not just live but to survive.

- **How do I get Spiritual Intimacy in my marriage?**

- **Study the bible together-** Set times and dates where you are both alone studying the bible together.
- **Discuss the word of God-** Share with each other what the word is teaching to you and how what you both are studying helped you the following day.
- **Pray together-** Make it a point to pray in the morning together and pray in before you go to bed at night. Ensure that this prayers includes holding hands, touching and agreeing through prayer. "A Marriage That Prays Together, Stays Together!"
- **Accountability-** You must have a level of accountability in your marriage, so that when begins to fall from this connection of spiritual growth, give each other spiritual correction and likewise when you see deeper growth complement each other in the same manner.
- **Reflect on your blessings-** This is a time set for you to thank God for the things he's done that week for you and your

marriage and family. Allow this time to be a time of praise and thanksgiving.

- **Spiritual Mentors-** It is important that you find spiritual mentors for your marriage, in some cases this is your pastor and his wife but doesn't have to be. This mentoring couple is who God has ordained to lead your marriage in the right direction to the next level, through being an example, spiritual wisdom and prayer.
- **Speak Life-** Begin to speak life into your marriage, speak greatness into your life, speak increase into your marriage, speak overflow into your marriage, and speak God's will into your marriage.
- **What are you waiting for SPEAK!!!!**

If you are making time to physical intimacy in your marriage, you need to be making time to have spiritual Intimacy in your marriage because once the physical man wears down, there must be a spiritual being that holds you both together.

- **Emotional In-to-me-see-** We must first understand that to have this level we must first be able to see each other's lives, dreams and goals. We must know each other's strengths and weaknesses in life and aware of each other's fears and hopes in life. This level comes with a high level of TRUST & COMMUNICATION that EMPOWERS you both to share the deepest parts of yourselves because you feel accepted, respected and loved in the eyes of your spouse because they accept you as you are, struggles and all, failures and all.

A marriage without Emotional Intimacy will be a marriage headed for destruction, a marriage living in a home lifeless allowing the home and bedroom to become smaller and smaller until it becomes so small that the husband & wife find themselves talking about separation and possibly divorce. This level requires that you are secure within yourself, your emotions, ensuring that your past has been closed off and dealt with and make it a point to be the person that your spouse feels safe with, allowing them to confide in you about anything that is going on with them. Be sure to deal with conflicts as soon as they happen, these things tend to be overlooked and swept under the rug and then the smallest issue arises and it becomes the issue that knocks over the table and exposes all the hurt, pain and strain that was never dealt with in the past.

Never stopped considering each other's feelings because once you do, your marriage will end up in the emotional ice age stage and that stage is hard to recover from because it will take a high level of fire to melt the ice that has caused you to be cold towards each other. Your marriage maybe in danger of this Ice Age stage if any of the following apply:

- **No touching-** When there's no touching you, you naturally lose the sense of feeling for each other.
- **No Kissing-** Remember your first kiss and how it made you think of your spouse that whole night. Kissing is a very important part of Intimacy.
- **No talking-** Every car ride is silent, every dinner date is silent and the home is very silent outside of the TV's that you both are watching in different rooms. If there is no communication, then there is no Emotional connection in your marriage. This will cause your first real communication in years to be on the subject of divorce.

Marriage of Pearls

- **Misunderstanding each other's needs-** This happens when you lose touch and connection with each other and neither of you know what the other really needs to make them feel needed, loved and healed. Because you haven't been communicating and your marriage has been in silent travail to quite some time now.

- **Love has left your eyes-** The person that you fell in love with is not the person you are not seeing right now. You see a person that you hate to be around, a person that you feel you hardly even know any more, a person that doesn't kindle your fire anymore and a person that you can't stand to look at anymore.

- **Sex has lost its pleasure-** You no longer desire to have sex and when you do, you feel like it's a chore and not love making, there is no foreplay, only let's get it over with, afterwards you take a shower in hopes of erasing the filth you feel off of you in a steamy shower. Once you emerge from the shower there is no after sex intimacy, no holding, no kissing, no rubbing, no sleeping on your spouse's chest, the bed only gets smaller and the king size bed you sleep in now feels like a twin bed in the dirtiest motel off the highway.

<u>You must put TRSUT, APPRECIATION, and CLOSENESS & COMMUNICATION back in your marriage for it to survive the ICE AGE STAGE!!!</u>

- **Don Meredith explains that God's design for sex builds unselfishness:**

God steps boldly to the point, finishing any faint-hearted commitment to the sexual relationship once and for all. My body is not mine, but my mate's. I am here to please. Hereafter, to demand rights over my body is to disagree with God's instruction. God makes sex a sacrificial act that is redemptive, in that it gets my eyes off my needs and onto the needs of my mate.

This literally means that there is/has to be mutual submission in the bedroom in order to please God and this happens to a husband and wife alone and not with others.

Exodus 20:14 **New International Version (NIV)**
[14] "You shall not commit adultery.

- **How does Jesus expand the definition of adultery?**

Our thought lives are where we so often sin. Perhaps you have never had a sexual relationship outside of marriage in the physical sense, but you may have enjoyed the thoughts. In God's eyes you are guilty. Sin begins in our thoughts and in our hearts. We must watch our thought lives so that we do not act upon what we think. As sinful thoughts build up, we may act on them; however, the thoughts themselves are enough to make us guilty.

Men desire intimacy just as we women do, so if they cannot receive it from their wives, they will often search for it elsewhere. H. Norman Wright gives us some insight concerning this.

- For women, sex is only one means of intimacy out of many and not always the best one. For many men, sex is the only expression of intimacy.

  Men tend to compress the meaning of intimacy into the sex act and when they don't have that outlet, they can become frustrated and upset. Why? Because they're cut off from the only source of closeness they know. Men are interested in closeness and intimacy but they have different ways of defining and expressing it.

H. Norman Wright

- One of the differences between husbands and wives is illustrated by their attitudes toward sex when they are physically tired. Sex is usually the last thing a wife wants when she's tired, but it provides her husband with the relaxation he needs for restoring sleep. Some women prefer sex at night while some men prefer to begin the day with this gratifying experience. Another difference is that after a quarrel a woman looks for words of reconciliation, but a man often looks for sex to heal the breach and restore the oneness with his wife. Someone stated the difference this way: "A man gives love for sex; a woman gives sex for love."

Jill Renich

- A wife may demonstrate her love in innumerable other ways but it is often negated by her rejection, or lack of enjoyment of sex. To a man, sex is the most meaningful demonstration of love and self-worth. A husband's gift of sexual pleasure is full of meaning. It's a part of his own deepest person. How his wife receives him has a much more profound effect on him than most women realize. To receive him with joy and to share sexual pleasure builds into him a sense of being worthy, desirable and acceptable. To reject him, to tolerate him and to put him off as unimportant tears at the very center of his self-esteem.

Jill Renich

"For this cause a man shall leave his father and mother, and shall cleave to his wife; and the two shall become one flesh. This mystery is great; but I am speaking with reference to Christ and the church" **(Ephesians 5:31-32).**
But because of immoralities, let each man have his own wife, and let each woman have her own husband. **(1 Corinthians 7:2)**
Let the husband fulfill his duty to his wife, and likewise also the wife to her husband. **(1 Corinthians 7:3)**
The wife does not have authority over her own body, but the husband does; and likewise also the husband does not have authority over his own body, but the wife does. **(1 Corinthians 7:4)**
But one who is married is concerned about the things of the world, how he may please his wife, but one who is married is concerned about the things of the world, how she may please her husband. **(1 Corinthians 7:33-34)**
Husbands, love your wives, just as Christ also loved the church and gave Himself up for her; that He might sanctify her, having cleansed her by the washing of water with the word, that He might present to Himself the church in all her glory, having no spot or wrinkle or any such thing; but that she should be holy and blameless" **(Ephesians 5:25-27).**
Mortify therefore your members which are upon the earth; fornication, uncleanness, inordinate affection, evil concupiscence, and covetousness, which is idolatry: Colossians 3:5

Experience Spiritual Intimacy While You Make Love!!!

Chapter 19

Discerning and destroying the Spirit Husband & Spirit Wife

In this chapter we will reveal the different types of "Spiritual Husbands/Wives" but before we get started in this chapter I must let you know, to destroy this spirit you must be born again and this is not a spirit that you want to take lightly because it will destroy everything around you and in you if not addressed through the power of God and pureness of being born again and use the authority through the blood of Jesus and the name of Jesus to cast this demon out of you, your spouse and your marriage and know the word of God that breaks/destroys any ties attached this spirit. In some cases, the person will need to reveal all their sex partners so that all soul ties can be commanded to leave your spouse and the sex-ties can then be broken and never to return. Each demon must be called out by name.

- **Demonic Sexual Attacks on women-** This may come from or even be caused by sexual sins, such as witchcraft spells, curses of lust, sensuality, inherited curses that were never broken from past generations and please understand these spirits can also attached itself to children.

- **Demonic Sexual Attacks on Men-** This may be caused by the same as the one caused by the women, but, we can overcome by the powerful blood of Jesus. All we have to do is be faithful over a few things and do our very best to live a Holy life style pleasing to God. Have faith in God and the word and in God!

When one commits fornication or Adultery, it is very important that you and your spouse understand that every curse and demonic spirits that were attached to them will transfer the next person they have sexual intercourse with. Sex is one of the most powerful and easiest ways a demon can be transferred to someone. That is why it is so important that WE break the soul-ties with our spirit husbands and spirit wives, these people have committed sexual sin with knowing or unknowingly. If you don't destroy the seed of this spirit, it can/will always return and pray with Psalm 91 for protection while destroying the seed. If this spirit is not dealt with the following witchcraft can/will produce in your marriage.

1. Someone in the marriage will become hateful and then you both will end up hating each other and you will never know why.
2. There will be a season where there is a anger, bitterness, hatred, regret and so much more hindrances that will draw you and your spouse far apart from each other into different places in your spirit and in life places there by the witch or warlock that is working against your marriage.
3. Familiar spirits will be unloosed into your marriage that will be begin hindering any emission of semen.
4. Your spouse's penis will become flabby and he will not desire to have sex with anyone but the one he has the soul-tie with. YES!!! "JUST THAT ONE WOMAN" is ALL he will ever desire and there is nothing you can do to attract him back you until this soul-tie is broken off of him forever.
5. The semen in your husband will not be fertile and able to produce.
6. Your wife's genital will become narrow and in some cases it will even close up. This can cause several dreams such as: demonic dreams, swimming or seeing a river or ocean in your dreams, missing your menstrual cycle in your dream, desiring a baby and a

family in your dreams, having a man who truly loves you in your dreams, anger towards your current spouse in your dreams, loss of unborn child in your dreams and even dreams of sexual encounters with friend at work that you are very close to but never thought of in that way.

- **Different Types of Spirit Husbands/Wives**

1. **The Resident Spirit Husband/Wife-** This spirit will seem to be making love to you and they will depart from for the rest of the day and return to you at night to do it all again.

2. **The Physical spirit Husband/Wife-** This spirit will go with you everywhere and never leave your side even for a second, this spirit will block things in the atmosphere that was meant to bless you or your spouse. They come to destroy/block favor on your life and marriage and this spirit becomes very jealous of your spouse and will seek to cause them harm. **"DESTROY THIS SPIRIT NOW!!!"**

3. **Territorial Spirit Husband/Wife-** This spirit will always stay in the area in which you live to protect their territory.

4. **Hermaphrodite Spirit Husband/Wife-** This spirit seeks to sleep with both the husband and the wife.

5. **Hidden Spirit Husband/Wife-** The spirit doesn't desire or even seek to sleep with anyone, instead this spirit's main goal is to cause sickness and withhold any breakthroughs that may have been released to you and your spouse.

6. **Masquerading Spirit Husband/Wife-** This spirit is very good at manipulating your mind and spirit by using the face of your spouse or even someone they know you have a secret desire for and have no will power to resist them. That is why it is very important that we do not lust after someone other than our spouses, this lust will used against us in the spirit realm and we will never see it coming until it is far too late.

7. **Multiple Spirit Husband/Wife-** This spirit is very dangerous because once this spirit has found its way into you, they go and bring other demonic spirits with it to have sex with you in the form of gang rape and will bring so many problems that you will never be able to explain. You will find yourself always seeking to have multiple partners at the same time and your spouse will not be able to satisfy you anymore.

8. **Incestuous Spirit Husband/Wife-** This spirit is manifested when you have demonic parents that are tapping into the demonic realm and they marry you spiritually with the goal of tapping into and draining your glory. This spirit is most effective when the parents are active in witchcraft or Masonic societies.

9. **Transferred Spirit Husband/Wife-** This spirit is activated when you are using items that belong to someone else such as combs, brushes, shoes and using any items that belong to the former victim will cause this spirit to be transferred to you.

10. **Leviathan Spirit Husband/Wife-** This spirit is very powerful and destructive, just look in the book of Job, this spirit carry a high level of SR power, just ranking below Satan himself. This spirit is activated and powered through Pride and Marine activities and is very stubborn and hard to get rid of but if you or your spouse don't humble yourselves before the lord, this spirit will destroy everything in your life and will stop at nothing until everything you love is dead.

11. **Imagination Spirit Husband/Wife-** This spirit will have sex with you in your dreams and will make it to where you wake up and will not be sure if it really happened and you will begin to think that you're going crazy because you can't remember the dream.

12. **Animal Spirit Husband/Wife-** This spirit regardless if it is the husband or the wife will use animal to attack you in your dreams through the form of sex and you feel like you are

really having sex with an animal and it will become so intense it will be hard for you to resist the animal sex in your dreams.

13. **Bloodline Spirit Husband/Wife-** This spirit travels through your bloodline going all the way back to the first marriage that was cursed in your family and will use those curses to destroy your marriage.

14. **Spirit Husband/Wife Masturbation-** This spirit has its greatest strength pornography and in marriages where there is little to no sexual contact in the marriage. This spirit will have men and women pleasuring themselves through porn more than with their spouses and in most cases when they're doing this, they're spouses are either in the house or have just left the house a few minutes before they masturbate. This spirit also gets strength from past childhood issues such as molestation as a child, rape as a child or being introduced to porn at an early age.

Bluntly speaking, most women don't meet a decent guy and are always attracting the same dogs as before because of the sinful daily practices that are causing the spirit husband to be activated in their lives and God becomes unpleased with your sexual acts of self-pleasuring that you limited what kind of man God is able to send you. It's time that you destroy the Spirit Husband in your life by first repenting and then destroying all of your sexual toys that are sitting in your top drawer or hidden in your closet and most of these toys, your own husband don't even know that you have them.

Remove everything from your house that causes you to sin in a sexual manner, rather it's physical or mental, remove it all, including movies and music.

Deliverance Scriptures Against Spiritual husband/wife marine spirits

- Isaiah 55:11 "So shall my word be that goeth forth out of my mouth: it shall not return unto me void, but it shall accomplish that which I please, and it shall prosper in the thing whereto I sent it."

- Joshua 5:9 "This day have I rolled away the reproach of Egypt from off you." Isaiah 54:5 "For thy Maker *is* thine husband; the LORD of hosts *is* his name; and thy Redeemer the Holy One of Israel; The God of the whole earth shall he be called." [Therefore if **Jesus** is your husband, then legally and according to Him, you cannot have any other marine husband or wife]

  - 1 Corinthians 6: 17 "But he that is joined unto the Lord is one spirit." [Therefore if you are one with God, you cannot be joined with any other god].

  - Isaiah 54:14 "…thou shall be far from oppression: for thou shall not fear: and from terror; for it shall not come near thee"

  - Isaiah 54: 17 "No weapon formed against you shall prosper, and every tongue *which* rises against you in judgment. You shall condemn. This *is* the heritage of the servants of the Lord, and their righteousness *is* from Me, Says the Lord."

  - Isaiah 54:4 "Fear not; for thou shalt not be ashamed: neither be thou confounded; for thou shalt not be put to shame: for thou shalt forget the shame of thy youth, and shalt not remember the reproach of thy widowhood anymore."

  - Isaiah 54:15 "Behold, they shall surely gather together, but not by me: whosoever shall gather together against thee shall fall for thy sake."

  - 1 John 4:4 "Ye are of God, little children, and have overcome them: because greater is he that is in you, than he that is in the world."

Chapter 20

Admire your Brides Beauty at all times!!!

Song of Solomon 4 English Standard Version (ESV)

1 Behold, you are beautiful, my love,
  behold, you are beautiful!
Your eyes are doves
  behind your veil.
Your hair is like a flock of goats
  leaping down the slopes of Gilead.
² Your teeth are like a flock of shorn ewes
  that have come up from the washing,
all of which bear twins,
  and not one among them has lost its young.
³ Your lips are like a scarlet thread,
  and your mouth is lovely.
Your cheeks are like halves of a pomegranate
  behind your veil.
⁴ Your neck is like the tower of David,
  built in rows of stone;[a]
on it hang a thousand shields,
  all of them shields of warriors.
⁵ Your two breasts are like two fawns,
  twins of a gazelle,
  that graze among the lilies.
⁶ Until the day breathes
  and the shadows flee,

I will go away to the mountain of myrrh
  and the hill of frankincense.
7 You are altogether beautiful, my love;
  there is no flaw in you.
8 Come with me from Lebanon, my bride;
  come with me from Lebanon.
Depart[b] from the peak of Amana,
  from the peak of Senir and Hermon,
from the dens of lions,
  from the mountains of leopards.
9 You have captivated my heart, my sister, my bride;
  you have captivated my heart with one glance of your eyes,
  with one jewel of your necklace.
10 How beautiful is your love, my sister, my bride!
  How much better is your love than wine,
  and the fragrance of your oils than any spice!
11 Your lips drip nectar, my bride;
  honey and milk are under your tongue;
  the fragrance of your garments is like the fragrance of Lebanon.
12 A garden locked is my sister, my bride,
  a spring locked, a fountain sealed.
13 Your shoots are an orchard of pomegranates
  with all choicest fruits,
  henna with nard,
14 nard and saffron, calamus and cinnamon,
  with all trees of frankincense,
myrrh and aloes,
  with all choice spices—
15 a garden fountain, a well of living water,
  and flowing streams from Lebanon.
16 Awake, O north wind,
  and come, O south wind!
Blow upon my garden,
  let its spices flow.

Together in the Garden of Love

Let my beloved come to his garden,
  and eat its choicest fruits.

Acknowledgements

Before we end, I wanted to take the time to mention some people who have been very instrumental in my life and my walk with God. First to my wife, you have been there in support of me through it all, even when others gave up, you stayed right there in the fight with me and you never gave up on me and I will always love you for the woman, wife and mother that you are! To the my Healing Waters family, you all are the best and you all always push me to use my strengths and anointing from God and I thank each and everyone one of you for your support and lessons you've taught me.

About The Author

DuJuan S Boyd

established and is Senior Pastor at Healing Waters Worship & Deliverance Center in Indianapolis, IN. He is also the founder of a Non-Profit counseling center in Indianapolis, IN "Healing Emergence Family & Marriage Counseling." As a speaker, preacher and teacher, he has empowered many to discover gifts and purpose in life and helped them to develop to their fullest potential. He has counseled and mended many marriages through the knowledge and power of God. He and his wife Jackie have 3 children and 1 grand –child, a Husky named Luke and DuJuan and his family reside in Indianapolis, IN.

For booking information call 317-919-4754/email: Dujuansboyd@gmail.com

Pure Thoughts Publishing, LLC

www.PureThoughtsPublishingllc.com